200 Years of American Graphic Art

In CONGRESS, July 4, 1776.

A DECLARATION

BY THE REPRESENTATIVES OF·THE

UNITED STATES OF AMERICA,

IN GENERAL CONGRESS ASSEMBLED.

WHEN in the Course of human Events, it becomes necessary for one People to dissolve the Political Bands which have connected them with another, and to assume among the Powers of the Earth, the separate and equal Station to which the Laws of Nature and of Nature's God entitle them, a decent Respect to the Opinions of Mankind requires that they should declare the causes which impel them to the Separation.

We hold these Truths to be self-evident, that all Men are created equal, that they are endowed by their Creator with certain unalienable Rights, that among these are Life, Liberty, and the Pursuit of Happiness—That to secure these Rights, Governments are instituted among Men, deriving their just Powers from the Consent of the Governed, that whenever any Form of Government becomes destructive of these Ends, it is the Right of the People to alter or to abolish it, and to institute new Government, laying its Foundation on such Principles, and organizing its Powers in such Form, as to them shall seem most likely to effect their Safety and Happiness. Prudence, indeed, will dictate that Governments long established should not be changed for light and transient Causes; and accordingly all Experience hath shewn, that Mankind are more disposed to suffer, while Evils are sufferable, than to right themselves by abolishing the Forms to which they are accustomed. But when a long Train of Abuses and Usurpations, pursuing invariably the same Object, evinces a Design to reduce them under absolute Despotism, it is their Right, it is their Duty, to throw off such Government, and to provide new Guards for their future Security. Such has been the patient Sufferance of these Colonies; and such is now the Necessity which constrains them to alter their former Systems of Government. The History of the present King of Great-Britain is a History of repeated Injuries and Usurpations, all having in direct Object the Establishment of an absolute Tyranny over these States. To prove this, let Facts be submitted to a candid World.

He has refused his Assent to Laws, the most wholesome and necessary for the public Good.

He has forbidden his Governors to pass Laws of immediate and pressing Importance, unless suspended in their Operation till his Assent should be obtained; and when so suspended, he has utterly neglected to attend to them.

He has refused to pass other Laws for the Accommodation of large Districts of People, unless those People would relinquish the Right of Representation in the Legislature, a Right inestimable to them, and formidable to Tyrants only.

He has called together Legislative Bodies at Places unusual, uncomfortable, and distant from the Depository of their public Records, for the sole Purpose of fatiguing them into Compliance with his Measures.

He has dissolved Representative Houses repeatedly, for opposing with manly Firmness his Invasions on the Rights of the People.

He has refused for a long Time, after such Dissolutions, to cause others to be elected; whereby the Legislative Powers, incapable of Annihilation, have returned to the People at large for their exercise; the State remaining in the mean time exposed to all the Dangers of Invasion from without, and Convulsions within.

He has endeavoured to prevent the Population of these States; for that Purpose obstructing the Laws for Naturalization of Foreigners; refusing to pass others to encourage their Migrations hither, and raising the Conditions of new Appropriations of Lands.

He has obstructed the Administration of Justice, by refusing his Assent to Laws for establishing Judiciary Powers.

He has made Judges dependent on his Will alone, for the Tenure of their Offices, and the Amount and Payment of their Salaries.

He has erected a Multitude of new Offices, and sent hither Swarms of Officers to harrass our People, and eat out their Substance.

He has kept among us, in Times of Peace, Standing Armies, without the consent of our Legislatures.

He has affected to render the Military independent of and superior to the Civil Power.

He has combined with others to subject us to a Jurisdiction foreign to our Constitution, and unacknowledged by our Laws; giving his Assent to their Acts of pretended Legislation:

FOR quartering large Bodies of Armed Troops among us:

FOR protecting them, by a mock Trial, from Punishment for any Murders which they should commit on the Inhabitants of these States:

FOR cutting off our Trade with all Parts of the World:

FOR imposing Taxes on us without our Consent:

FOR depriving us, in many Cases, of the Benefits of Trial by Jury:

FOR transporting us beyond Seas to be tried for pretended Offences:

FOR abolishing the free System of English Laws in a neighbouring Province, establishing therein an arbitrary Government, and enlarging its Boundaries, so as to render it at once an Example and fit Instrument for introducing the same absolute Rule into these Colonies:

FOR taking away our Charters, abolishing our most valuable Laws, and altering fundamentally the Forms of our Governments:

FOR suspending our own Legislatures, and declaring themselves invested with Power to legislate for us in all Cases whatsoever.

He has abdicated Government here, by declaring us out of his Protection and waging War against us.

He has plundered our Seas, ravaged our Coasts, burnt our Towns, and destroyed the Lives of our People.

He is, at this Time, transporting large Armies of foreign Mercenaries to compleat the Works of Death, Desolation, and Tyranny, already begun with circumstances of Cruelty and Perfidy, scarcely paralleled in the most barbarous Ages, and totally unworthy the Head of a civilized Nation.

He has constrained our fellow Citizens taken Captive on the high Seas to bear Arms against their Country, to become the Executioners of their Friends and Brethren, or to fall themselves by their Hands.

He has excited domestic Insurrections amongst us, and has endeavoured to bring on the Inhabitants of our Frontiers, the merciless Indian Savages, whose known Rule of Warfare, is an undistinguished Destruction, of all Ages, Sexes and Conditions.

IN every stage of these Oppressions we have Petitioned for Redress in the most humble Terms: Our repeated Petitions have been answered only by repeated Injury. A Prince, whose Character is thus marked by every act which may define a Tyrant, is unfit to be the Ruler of a free People.

NOR have we been wanting in Attentions to our British Brethren. We have warned them from Time to Time of Attempts by their Legislature to extend an unwarrantable Jurisdiction over us. We have reminded them of the Circumstances of our Emigration and Settlement here. We have appealed to their native Justice and Magnanimity, and we have conjured them by the Ties of our common Kindred to disavow these Usurpations, which, would inevitably interrupt our Connections and Correspondence. They too have been deaf to the Voice of Justice and of Consanguinity. We must, therefore, acquiesce in the Necessity, which denounces our Separation, and hold them, as we hold the rest of Mankind, Enemies in War, in Peace, Friends.

WE, therefore, the Representatives of the UNITED STATES OF AMERICA, in GENERAL CONGRESS, Assembled, appealing to the Supreme Judge of the World for the Rectitude of our Intentions, do, in the Name, and by Authority of the good People of these Colonies, solemnly Publish and Declare, That these United Colonies are, and of Right ought to be, FREE AND INDEPENDENT STATES; that they are absolved from all Allegiance to the British Crown, and that all political Connection between them and the State of Great-Britain, is and ought to be totally dissolved; and that as FREE AND INDEPENDENT STATES, they have full Power to levy War, conclude Peace, contract Alliances, establish Commerce, and to do all other Acts and Things which INDEPENDENT STATES may of right do. And for the support of this Declaration, with a firm Reliance on the Protection of divine Providence, we mutually pledge to each other our Lives, our Fortunes, and our sacred Honor.

Signed by ORDER and in BEHALF of the CONGRESS,

JOHN HANCOCK, PRESIDENT.

ATTEST.
CHARLES THOMSON, SECRETARY.

PHILADELPHIA: PRINTED BY JOHN DUNLAP.

The first printed Declaration of Independence in reduced facsimile (original type form measured twelve by seventeen inches). It was printed by John Dunlap of Philadelphia, and it was this setting that was read before Washington's army.

200 Years of American Graphic Art

A Retrospective Survey of the Printing Arts and Advertising since the Colonial Period

*by Clarence P. Hornung
and Fridolf Johnson*

GEORGE BRAZILLER   New York

For information address the publisher:

GEORGE BRAZILLER, INC.
One Park Avenue
New York, N.Y. 10016

International Standard Book Number: 0–8076–0791–6
Library of Congress Catalog Card Number: 75–10966

Printed in the U.S.A.

PREFACE

THE TERM GRAPHIC ARTS is defined as pertaining to painting, drawing, engraving, or *any other art* which expresses ideas by means of lines, marks, or characters impressed or printed on a surface. As a definition this is clear enough; not so clear are the limits to be imposed upon the present survey of graphic arts, which bypasses completely the arts of painting and prints. The crude and largely untutored graphic efforts of our Colonial forefathers have been transformed, within a number of generations, into a discipline which, decade after decade, has continued to develop in skills, complexity, and wider horizons.

Aesthetically, American graphic arts have alternately reached high levels of excellence and descended to deep troughs of tastelessness. Fluctuations in public taste have been attended, and often created, by advances in technology. Printing, publishing, advertising, and reproductive techniques have become so bound up with graphic arts that a survey of this kind requires brief excursions into these domains to make clear their relationships. We have emphasized their early history as material unfamiliar or inaccessible to the average reader.

When the proposal to undertake this study was first made the authors were intrigued with its possibilities and excited about the opportunity to share, in some small measure, the observance of this bicentennial occasion. The life and soul of our American heritage in its beginnings is being told and retold in countless ways in order to bring into better perspective the present-day order of things. Events are being reenacted; historical episodes are being recreated; books, pamphlets, and important documents are being reprinted. Every phase of our country's origins is being reintroduced to an eager public attuned to listen and learn.

But the task before us loomed almost insurmountable. Literally hundreds of volumes have been issued in the past, covering, so it seemed, every facet of this fascinating bit of Americana and dealing with both written and iconographic aspects. Our preliminary surveys indicated that to do full justice to the subject, we should allow a number of years for diligent research, compilation of pictorial material, design, and production of the finished book. The mass of relevant data could fill a ten-volume encyclopedia totaling at least five thousand pages, and then not exhaust every angle worth exploring. However, we agreed to accept the restrictive conditions imposed by a tight time schedule and a compact volume as both a challenge and a stimulus.

The authors have aimed to create a book that will engage the reader and inspire him to further studies. It does not provide instruction in the involved science of advertising and marketing, nor does it delve into the intricacies of modern printing techniques and technology. Its text presents a selection of representative examples and discussion of general trends, offering highlights that serve to illuminate the larger subjects. The time periods or chapters have been subdivided by the dictates of material in hand and thus do not correspond to any accepted historical breakdown, except in a very general way.

Limitations of space preclude little more than passing mention of magazine and book illustration, the print in its many manifestations as an art form, and many, minor byways of graphic art represented by greeting cards, bookplates, book jackets, penmanship, calligraphy, various aspects of the corporate image including trademarks, packaging, annual reports, and the multitudinous facets of modern visual communications. It is our hope that by providing some tempting bits and pieces we have encouraged the reader to delve deeper into a rich subject. He and she will find a guide to further exploration in the selective bibliography offered at the end of this volume.

C. P. H.

F. J.

ACKNOWLEDGMENTS

WE RECORD our thanks and indebtedness to the many libraries, institutions, and individuals who have generously helped in the compilation of this volume. Unfortunately, we have been able to use but a fraction of the wealth of illustrative material offered, because of the limitations imposed by a modest volume. For this, we offer regret.

The following institutions and their staffs have been most cooperative: American Antiquarian Society; American Institute of Graphic Arts; John Carter Brown Library; Davis Collection of Theatre Memorabilia; Ogden Goelet Collection; Historical Society of Pennsylvania; Library Company of Philadelphia; Library of Congress; New York Public Library; State Street Trust Company of Boston, Trusts and Estates, New York.

The bulk of the illustrations used are from the personal collections of the authors. Additional supplementary material has been provided by the following: Seymour Chwast; Paul Davis; Walter Einsel; Woody Gelman; Milton Glaser; Joseph Weiler.

A special acknowledgment is due Edward M. Gottschall, executive director of the American Institute of Graphic Arts, for his deep interest and helpful comments throughout the course of this project. His personal enthusiasm has been most appreciated. The authors express their deepest gratitude to Julianne J. deVere for editorial assistance and help in countless ways that have expedited the course of production. And to George Braziller whose confidence from the outset has provided our greatest incentive.

CONTENTS

200 Years of American Graphic Art

1

Even after the departure of the Dutch governors and the takeover by the British in 1664, the burghers in New York were still predominantly Dutch, most of whom spoke little English. Proclamations were read aloud so that all could understand the latest municipal regulations. Engraving, after a drawing by Paul Frenzeny which first appeared in *Harper's Weekly*, September 23, 1882.

1640-1776

COLONIAL PROLOGUE

THE HISTORY of graphic art in America actually began with the establishment of the first Colonial printing press in 1639. Before that time—and long after—every scrap of paper for drawing or writing had to be imported; artists were uncommon and too occupied with more vital concerns. Without printers or newspapers there was no advertising. News from abroad was always obsolete by several weeks; local news was spread by gossip, official information by town crier.

Every bit of ephemeral printing as well as books to nourish the soul and instruct the young had to come from Europe. Books of more popular appeal were no doubt imported in quantities and read until they fell apart. The authorities frowned on any reading matter construed as frivolous or likely to deflect mind or heart from stern purpose; there was little room or time for the amenities of leisure or unproductive entertainment.

The people who colonized the New World came of their own free will. The first to come had room in their ships for little more than the bare necessities and the victuals to sustain them during the long voyage. The moment they set foot on our soil they were faced with the task of providing shelter as well as food just to stay alive. A leaflet printed in London, 1622, lists the essentials for a family or single man intending to go to Jamestown, Virginia. It includes wearing apparel, such staples as "Meale, pease, aquavitae, Oyle, and Vineger"; armor, weapons, and powder; a large assortment of tools and household utensils. There is no mention of furniture or luxuries.

The settlers were predominantly British. Other nations were represented, but by 1664 the Dutch and Swedish colonies in New York, New Jersey, and Delaware had begun to merge into the English community. The first Germans to arrive in 1693 took root in Germantown, Pennsylvania, and managed to retain a large part of their individuality in succeeding decades.

Various geographic and social conditions inevitably brought about a natural division of the land into three parts: New England, clustered along

Massachusetts Bay; the Middle Colonies, centered in what was to become Philadelphia; and the Southern Colonies along the fertile coast of Virginia.

The New Englanders, forced to contend with inclement weather and the inhospitable, rock-ribbed soil, had the hardest time. The Mayflower landed at Plymouth in December, 1620, with but 102 people—eighteen of them women—and within five months half of them had succumbed to the hardships of the first winter. To the north was but "a hidious and desolate wilderness, full of wild beasts and willd [sic] men." Building their houses close together for protection and comfort, they naturally turned to the sea for sustenance and commerce. They started a brisk fur trade with the Indians, even bartering the beaver skirts off the loins of their squaws who, Winthrop wrote, "tied boughs about them, but with great shame-facedness." Cod and trees were plentiful, and they sent cargoes of clapboard to England in exchange for necessities they were unable to provide for themselves.

Sermons and daily meditations on widely shared religious beliefs and the soul's salvation nurtured a desire for learning. Though people were grimly practical, their intellectual level was high, and there was a powerful impetus toward the founding of schools. In 1639 Dorchester, Massachusetts, already had a public school supported directly by taxes, and in that same year Harvard College was chartered and named in honor of John Harvard, who had bequeathed to it his library of some four hundred volumes and a considerable sum of money. It was also in this year that the College authorities sponsored the first printing press to be set up in British America.

The Middle Colonies were made up of a population much less homogeneous than that of New England. The rich soil encouraged extensive farming, and the easily navigable waterways promoted the growth of small towns where industries could flourish. Much of the wealth was drawn to the larger towns; especially to Philadelphia, which a century later became famous for its furniture craftsmen, who worked mainly in the popular Chippendale style. Houses were built with an eye to comfort and elegance, well stocked with books and fine appointments.

The character of the Southern Colonies was early determined by land grants from the British Crown to favored individuals and companies. Virginia is divided naturally into strips of land connected by water, leading to its being parceled out into huge cotton and tobacco plantations. Towns and villages were superfluous in such an economy. The possession of land became the basis of wealth and social standing. The wide dispersal of country mansions fostered an almost feudal existence among the landowners with their great homes and armies of servants. Slavery began in Virginia, at Jamestown in 1619, when, as John Rolfe reported, "there came a dutch man of warre that sold us Twenty Negars."

The first to bring a printing press to British America was the Reverend Jose Glover, believed to have had some connection with Harvard College. On his second trip to the New World, in the summer of 1638, he brought a press, paper, and type. Also on board was a locksmith named Stephen Daye to help set up the press at the college. Glover died during the voyage "of a fever," and his widow bought a large house in New-Town—later called Cambridge—and the Harvard authorities provided a home for Daye and his family. Though Daye was not a printer, the press was set up in his house and operation of it began immediately.

According to John Winthrop's *Journal,* the first item to issue from the press was the "freeman's Oath," and the second an "Almanack for New England by Mr. William Peirce, Mariner." No copies of these are known. The third item was *The Whole Booke of Psalmes Faithfully Translated into English Metre,* commonly known as the *Bay Psalm Book.* Of the first edition of 1,700 copies only eleven have survived. It was finished in 1640, and its 294 pages full of small type reveal all the sins of crude workmanship.

It is difficult to believe that Stephen Daye was capable of operating the press, let alone setting type and reading proof. He was uneducated, and surviving letters written by him reveal an astonishing conception of orthography. There are those who insist, and with good reason, that though Stephen undoubtedly set up the press, the honor of being our first printer should go to Daye's son Matthew who, though only eighteen at the time, had had perhaps four years training as a printer's apprentice in England. Stephen Daye's interest turned to real estate; Matthew went on printing, but his name does not appear on any imprint until 1647, and then only once—in an almanac for that year, of which only one copy has been preserved.

Matthew died a bachelor May 10, 1649. His successor at the press was Samuel Green, then thirty-four years of age. Though not a printer he did very well, and members of the Green family went on printing until at least 1839. The press itself was moved several times, suffered hard use and later neglect, and finally came to rest at the Vermont Historical Society at Montpelier.

The first Colonial presses were not unlike those used in Europe a century before, based on the principle of the wine screw-press. A strong pull on a bar attached to the screw exerted great downward pressure of an oblong block, called the *platen,* upon a sheet of paper laid over a previously inked form of type.

The frame of the press was necessarily built of heavy timbers. The *bed,* upon which the type form was laid, ran on tracks which extended sufficiently far from under the platen to make the form accessible for inking and adjustments. Hinged to this movable bed was the *tympan,* with guides for positioning the paper over the form. Hinged to the outer edge of the tympan was the *frisket,* somewhat similar to a mat for a picture, which, when folded down over paper and tympan, protected the margins from accidental smearing.

The type was set, letter by letter, in a composing stick held in the hand, and then transferred, printing end up, to a smooth composing stone. When the form was completely set up and spacing material inserted, it was "locked up" by wedging it within a sturdy frame, or *chase,* and placed on the movable carriage of the press.

Inking the type before each impression was a laborious process, and was generally done by a boy. In each hand he held a leather ball stuffed with wool and attached to a wooden handle. Using a patting motion, with the ink balls he transferred fresh ink from an inking board to the form, making sure all the type had received a film of ink. Oddly enough, the idea of spreading ink by means of a roller was not realized until about 1829.

Meanwhile the paper had been placed on the tympan, and when inking had been completed, tympan and frisket were folded down over the form and the carriage run under the platen. Providing the boy had done a good job of inking and the pressman was strong enough to exert sufficient "squeeze," a fairly satisfactory impression was obtained. A form larger than the platen would require two such squeezes, one for each end of the sheet. Then the procedure began all over again. In spite of the complexity of the process, two men working together could produce an average of 240 two-squeeze impressions per hour. As paper was scarce, printers seldom allowed themselves the luxury of discards unless an impression was quite unreadable.

In 1640, there were about thirty thousand settlers along the coast from Maine to Virginia; nearly half of these were in the Massachusetts Bay Colony. Virginia had eight or nine thousand; and at Jamestown the second Colonial press was set up by William Nuthead in 1682. Other presses followed gradually. Besides Massachusetts and Virginia, in 1776 there was at least one printer—in order of precedence—in Maryland, New York, Connecticut, New Jersey, Rhode Island, South Carolina, North Carolina, New Hampshire, Delaware, Georgia, and Louisiana.

The first newspaper to appear in the colonies was *Publick Occurrences Both Forreign and Domestic,* issued in Boston by Benjamin Harris on September 25, 1690. It was a four-page leaflet, 6 × 9½ inches, crowded with small type set two columns to a page. The fourth page was left blank, presumably for Bostonians to write in other news of interest before forwarding to friends at a distance. It was promptly suppressed because it had been published "without the least Privity or Countenance of Authority."

Fourteen years were to elapse before the next recorded newspaper was issued. John Campbell, Postmaster of Boston, which now had a population of about ten thousand, founded what was to become the first regularly published American newspaper. "Published by authority," the *Boston News-Letter* first appeared in April, 1704, as a single leaf printed on both sides. Campbell also had the distinction of running the first newspaper advertisement in America: an offer of a reward for the return of two anvils "stolen from Mr. Shippen's wharf."

Benjamin Franklin (1706–1790) played a major role in the development of printing arts. His considerable abilities and business acumen made him a leader as printer and publisher as well as a dealer in ink, paper, and books. His *Poor Richard's Almanack* became famous.

The *Pennsylvania Gazette,* first issued in October, 1729, by Benjamin Franklin, was immediately successful and set a high standard of content and typography for later papers. It was Franklin, also, who published what may well be called the first American newspaper cartoon in the May, 1754, issue: the famous one-column cut of a snake divided into eight parts, with the legend, "Join, or Die."

Franklin was the first to conceive the idea of publishing a general magazine, with John Webb, an attorney, to be its editor. But Franklin's bitter rival, William Bradford, stole both the idea and the editor and succeeded in publishing his *American Magazine* in January, 1741, just three days before Franklin's own *General Magazine* appeared. Evidently the colonists were not ready for general periodical literature; Bradford issued only three numbers and Franklin six.

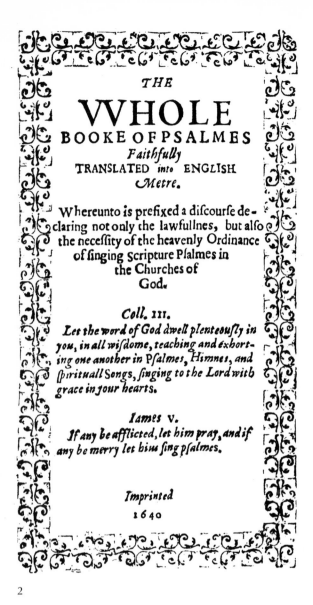

THE

WHOLE
BOOKE OF PSALMES
Faithfully
TRANSLATED *into* ENGLISH
Metre.

Whereunto is prefixed a discourse declaring not only the lawfullnes, but also
the necessity of the heavenly Ordinance
of singing Scripture Psalmes in
the Churches of
God.

Coll. III.

*Let the word of God dwell plenteously in
you, in all wisdome, teaching and exhort-
ing one another in Psalmes, Himnes, and
spirituall Songs, singing to the Lord with
grace in your hearts.*

Iames V.

*If any be afflicted, let him pray, and if
any be merry let him sing psalmes.*

Imprinted
1640

2

The Humble

PETITION
AND

ADDRESS
Of the General Court sitting at
Boston in *New-England*,
UNTO
The High and Mighty
PRINCE

CHARLES
THE SECOND.

And presented unto His Most-Gracious
Majesty *Feb.* 11. 1660.

Printed in the Year 1660.

3

A
PROCLAMATION

BY The *PRESIDENT* and *COUNCIL* of His Majesty's Territory & Dominion of *NEW-ENGLAND* in AMERICA.

WHEREAS His Most Excellent Majesty our Soveraign LORD *JAMES* the Second, King of England, Scotland, France and Ireland, Defender of the Faith &c. by COMMISSION or Letters Patents under His Great Seal of *England*, bearing Date the Eight day of *October* in the first *&c.* — of His Reign hath been graciously pleased to erect and constitute a PRESIDENT and COUNCIL to take Care of all His Territory and Dominion of *New-England* called the *Massachusetts Bay*, the Province of *New-Hampshire* & *Main*, and the *Narraganset Country*, otherwise called the *Kings-Province*, with all the Islands, Rights and Members thereunto appertaining, and to Order Rule and GOVERN the same according to the Rules, Methods and Regulations specified in the said Commission: Together with His Majesties Gracious Indulgence in matters of Religion.

...

GOD SAVE THE KING

BOSTON, in N. E. Printed by *Richard Pierce*, Printer to the Honourable His Majesties President and Council of this Government.

4

By royal proclamation, all type, ornaments, and the necessary cuts were imported from England. Since journeyman printers were all British, it follows that the prevailing typographic style resembled what was currently in vogue in the mother country. The first book printed in British America (2) was produced by Stephen Daye at Cambridge in 1640. Many royal petitions were printed and circulated throughout the colonies, typified by (3), issued in 1660. The first book printed in Virginia, also the first on the art of printing (5) is the work of William Parker, done at Williamsburg in 1730.

TYPOGRAPHIA.

AN

ODE,

ON

PRINTING.

Inscrib'd to the Honourable

WILLIAM GOOCH, *Esq;*

His Majesty's Lieutenant-Governor, and Commander in Chief of the Colony of *VIRGINIA.*

———— *Pleni sunt omnes Libri, plenæ sapientum voces, plena Exemplorum vetustas; quæ jacerent in Tenebris omnia, nisi Literarum Lumen accederet.*

Cic. Orat. pro Archia.

WILLIAMSBURG:

Printed by WILLIAM PARKS. M,DCC,XXX.

A

Brief History

OF THE

𝔓𝔢𝔮𝔲𝔬𝔱 𝔚𝔞𝔯:

Especially
Of the memorable *Taking* of their FORT at
MISTICK in CONNECTICUT
In

1 6 3 7.

Written by
Major *John Mason*,

A principal Actor therein, as then chief *Captain* and Commander of *Connecticut Forces.*

With an *Introduction* and some Explanatory *Notes*
By the Reverend
Mr. THOMAS PRINCE.

Psal. xliv. 1--3 *We have heard with our Ears, O GOD, our Fathers have told us, what WorkThou didst in their Days, in the times of old: How Thou dist drive out the Heathen with thy Hand, and plantedst Them: howThou did afflict the People and cast them out. For they got not the Land in Possession by their own Sword, neither did their own Arm save them: but thy right Hand, and thine Arm, and the Light of thy Countenance, because Thou hadst a Favour unto them.*
Psal. cii. 18. *This shall be written for theGeneration to come: and the People which shall be Created, shall Praise the LORD.*

BOSTON: Printed & Sold by. S. KNEELAND & T. GREEN
in Queen-street, 1736.

6

THE
HOLY BIBLE:
CONTAINING THE
OLD TESTAMENT
AND THE *NEW.*

Translated into the
INDIAN LANGUAGE
AND
Ordered to be Printed by the *Commissioners of the United Colonies*
in *NEW-ENGLAND*,

At the Charge, and with the Consent of the
CORPORATION IN ENGLAND
For the Propagation of the Gospel amongst the Indians
in New-England.

CAMBRIDGE:
Printed by *Samuel Green* and *Marmaduke Johnson.*
MDCLXIII.

7

Major *Mason's*
Brief HISTORY
OF THE
Pequot War.

8

Many colonial broadsides and volumes dealt with various aspects of the Indian problem. The Pequot War of 1637 was fully described (6, 8) in a book issued about a century later. The Church of England authorized a special translation of the Old Testament (7), designed to spread the Gospel among the natives. Set in the ever-popular Caslon Oldstyle (9), this broadside calls a conference in Maine to halt the French-inspired Indian raids.

A
CONFERENCE

Held at St. *George*'s in the County of *York*,
on the Twentieth Day of *September*, *Anno Regni Regis* G E O R G I I *Secundi*, *Magnæ Britanniæ Franciæ et Hiberniæ*, *Vicefimo Septimo*. Annoque Domini, 1 7 5 3.

B E T W E E N

Sir *William Pepperrell*, Baronet, *Jacob Wendell*, *Thomas Hubbard*, and *John Winflow*, Efqrs; and Mr. *James Bowdoin*.

C O M M I S S I O N E R S

Appointed by His E X C E L L E N C Y

W I L L I A M   S H I R L E Y, Efq;

Captain General and Governour in Chief, in and over His Majefty's Province of the *Maffachufetts-Bay* in *New-England*,

to Treat with the

Eastern Indians

of the one Part,
and the Indians of the *Penobfcott* Tribe
of the other Part.

B O S T O N in *N E W-E N G L A N D* :
Printed by **Samuel Kneeland**, Printer to the Honourable Houfe of
R E P R E S E N T A T I V E S.   1 7 5 3.

9

Tulley, 1 6 9 9.

A N

Almanack

For the Year of our Lord, *M DC XC IX.*
Being Third after Leap-Year,
and from the Creation,
5 6 4 8.
Wherein is Contained the Lunations, Courts, Spring Tides, Planets, Aſpects and Weather, the Riſing and Setting of the SUN, together with the Sun and Moons place, and time of Full Sea, or High-Water, with an account of the *Eclipſes*, Conjunctions, and other Configurations of the Cæleſtial Bodies.

Calculated for and fitted to the Meridian of Boſton in New-England, where the North Pole is Elevated 42.*gr.*30.*min.* But may indifferently ſerve any part of New-England.

By JOHN TULLEY.

Licenſed by Authority.

BOSTON, N. E. Printed by *Bartholomew Green*, and *John Allen* Sold at the Printing-Houſe at the South end of the Town. 1 6 9 9.

10

Poor Richard, 1733.

A N

Almanack

For the Year of Chriſt

1 7 3 3,

Being the Firſt after LEAP YEAR:

And makes ſince the Creation	Years
By the Account of the Eaſtern *Greeks*	7241
By the Latin Church, when ⊙ ent. ♈	6932
By the Computation of *W W*	5742
By the *Roman* Chronology	5682
By the *Jewiſh* Rabbies	5494

Wherein is contained

The Lunations, Eclipſes, Judgment of the Weather, Spring Tides, Planets Motions & mutual Aſpects, Sun and Moon's Riſing and Setting, Length of Days, Time of High Water, Fairs, Courts, and obſervable Days

Fitted to the Latitude of Forty Degrees, and a Meridian of Five Hours Weſt from *London*, but may without ſenſible Error ſerve all the adjacent Places, even from *Newfoundland* to *South-Carolina*.

By *RICHARD SAUNDERS*, Philom.

PHILADELPHIA:
Printed and ſold by *B FRANKLIN*, at the New Printing Office near the Market

11

Mon. March hath xxxi days.

My Love and I for Kiſſes play'd,
She would keep ſtakes, I was content,
But when I won ſhe would be paid;
This made me aſk her what ſhe meant:
Quoth ſhe, ſince you are in this wrangling vein,
Here take your Kiſſes, give me mine again.

1	5	Q. Caroline Nat.	11	♒	6	9	6	St. David
2	6		12	21	6	8	6	☽ riſ. 4 16 mo.
3	7	High ſpring tides.	1	♓	6	7	6	New ☽ 4 day,
4	G	4 Sund. Lent	2	20	6	5	6	at 10 at night.
5	2	7 * ſet 11 2	3	♈	6	4	6	*Let my reſpected*
6	3	Days 11 h. 54 m.	4	20	6	3	6	*friend* J. G.
7	4	*Wind and cloudy*	5	♉	6	2	6	☽ ſets 9 40 aft.
8	5	✱ ♂ ♀ *cold*	6	20	6	1	6	*Accept this hum-*
9	6	⊙ ent. ♈ then	6h	♊	6	0	6	*ble verſe of me.*
10	7	Spring Q begins	7	19	5	59	7	viz.
11	G	△ ♃ ☿ & makes	8	♋	5	58	7	Firſt Quarter
12	2	Eq. Day & Night	9	16	5	56	7	*Ingenious, learn-*
13	3	☌ ⊙ ♀ ☍ ♃ ♂	10	29	5	55	7	*ed, envy'd Youth,*
14	4	*Windy but warm*	10	♌	5	54	7	☽ ſets 3 morn.
15	5	Days incr. 3 h.	11	24	5	53	7	*Go on as thou'ſt*
16	6	7 * ſet 10 20	12	♍	5	52	7	*began;*
17	7	St. Patrick	1	19	5	51	7	*Even thy enemies*
18	G	Palm Sunday	2	♎	5	49	7	*take pride*
19	2	*March many wea-*	2h	13	5	48	7	Full ● 19 day
20	3	☌ ♄ ☿ *thers*	3	25	5	47	7	3 in the Morn.
21	4	*How he buffs, poor*	4	♏	5	46	7	☽ riſ 8 46 aft.
22	5	7 * ſet 10 0 *Fool!*	5	19	5	45	7	*That thou'rt*
23	6	Good Friday	6	♐	5	44	7	*their country*
24	7	*Now fair & clear*	6h	13	5	43	7	*man*
25	G	EASTER Day	7	24	5	42	7	
26	2	7 * ſet 9 45	8	♑	5	40	7	☽ riſ. 1 morn.
27	3	*High winds, with*	9	20	5	39	7	Laſt Quarter.
28	4	*ſome rain to the*	10	♒	5	37	7	*Hunger never*
29	5	☌ ⊙ ♄ *end*	10	16	5	35	7	*ſaw bad bread.*
30	6	☍ ♃ ♀	11	♓	5	34	7	Days incr. 3 38
31	7	7 * ſet 9 27	12	14	5	33	7	☽ riſ. 3 28

12

ΚΟΜΗΤΟΓΡΑΦΙΑ.

OR A
Diſcourſe Concerning
COMETS;

Wherein the Nature of BLAZING STARS
is Enquired into:

With an Hiſtorical Account of all the COMETS
which have appeared from the Beginning of the
World unto this preſent Year, M.DC.LXXXII.

Expreſſing

The Place in the Heavens, where they were ſeen,
Their Motion, Forms, Duration ; and the Remarkable Events which have followed
in the World, ſo far as they have been
by Learned Men Obſerved.

As alſo two SERMONS
Occaſioned by the late *Blazing Stars.*

By *INCREASE MATHER,* Teacher of a Church
at *Boſton* in *New-England.*

Pſal. 111. 2. *The works of the Lord are great, ſought
out of all them that have pleaſure therein.*
Amos 9. 6. *He buildeth his ſtories in the Heaven.*

BOSTON IN NEW-ENGLAND.
Printed by *S. G.* for *S. S.* And ſold by *J. Browning*
At the corner of the Priſon Lane next the Town-
Houſe 1683.

13

ANNO REGNI
GEORGII II.
REGIS
MAGNÆ BRITANNIÆ, FRANCIÆ, & HIBERNIÆ,
VICESIMO PRIMO.

At a GENERAL ASSEMBLY of the Colony of
New-Jerſey, continued by Adjournments to
the 17th Day of *November, Anno Dom.*
1747, and then begun and holden at *Bur-*
lington, being the fifth Sitting of the ſecond
Seſſion of this preſent Aſſembly.

PHILADELPHIA:
Printed by B. FRANKLIN, Printer to the King's
moſt excellent Majeſty for the Province of *New-Jerſey.*
M,DCC,XLVIII.

14

Two important books that have served the farm
folk since colonial times are the Bible and the
annually issued almanacs. The former offered to
cure the ills of the soul, the latter those of the
body. The farmer and his family pored over the
meaty wisdom contained in each new almanac
for news of the tides, sunrise and sunset, and
aspects of lunar movements. The title page of
the *Tulley Almanac* for 1699 (10) is enriched
with a border of printer's flowers. The discourse
on comets of 1683 (13) is decorated with woodcuts of local origin. The other examples are
the work of Ben Franklin.

Juſt Publiſhed,
And to be ſold by B. FRANKLIN, the following BOOKS,

I. THe POCKET ALMANACK,
for the Year 1745.

II. *PAMELA;* or *Virtue rewarded. In a*
Series of FAMILIAR LETTERS
from a beautiful young Damſel, to her Parents.
Now firſt Publiſhed, in order to cultivate the
Principles of Virtue *and* Religion *in the Minds*
of the Youth *of both Sexes.*
A Narrative which has its Foundation in Truth
and Nature *; and at the ſame time that it a-*
greeably entertains, by a Variety of curious
and affecting INCIDENTS, *is intirely diveſted*
of all thoſe Images, which, in too many Pie-
ces, calculated for Amuſement only, tend to
inflame the Minds they ſhould inſtruct.
Price 6 s.

III. A Preſervative from the Sins and Follies
of Childhood and Youth, *written by way of*
Queſtion and Anſwer. To which are added, ſome Relig-
ous and Moral Inſtructions, in Verſe. By I. Watts, D. D.
Price 8 d.

15

13

THE
New-England Courant.

[Nº 80

From MONDAY February 4. to MONDAY February 11. 1723.

The late Publisher of this Paper, finding so many Inconveniences would arise by his carrying the Manuscripts and publick News to be supervis'd by the Secretary, as to render his carrying it on unprofitable, has intirely dropt the Undertaking. The present Publisher having receiv'd the following Piece, desires the Readers to accept of it as a Preface to what they may hereafter meet with in this Paper.

Non ego mordaci distrinxi Carmine quenquam,
Nulla venenato Litera onista Joco est.

ONG has the Press groaned in bringing forth an hateful, but numerous Brood of Party Pamphlets, malicious Scribbles, and Billinsgate Ribaldry. The Rancour and bitterness it has unhappily infused into Mens' minds, and to what a Degree it has sowred and leaven'd the Tempers of Persons formerly esteemed some of the most sweet and affable, is too well known here, to need any further Proof or Representation of the Matter.

No generous and impartial Person then can blame the present Undertaking, which is designed purely for the Diversion and Merriment of the Reader. Pieces of Pleasancy and Mirth have a secret Charm in them to allay the Heats and Tumours of our Spirits, and to make a Man forget his restless Resentments. They have a strange Power to tune the harsh Disorders of the Soul, and reduce us to a serene and placid State of Mind.

The main Design of this Weekly Paper will be to entertain the Town with the most comical and diverting Incidents of Humane Life, which in so large a Place as *Boston*, will not fail of a universal Exemplification: Nor shall we be wanting to fill up these Papers with a grateful Interspersion of more serious Morals, which may be drawn from the most ludicrous and odd Parts of Life.

As for the Author, that is the next Question. But tho' we profess our selves ready to oblige the ingenious and courteous Reader with most Sorts of Intelligence, yet here we beg a Reserve. Nor will it be of any Manner of Advantage either to them or to the Writers, that their names should be published; and therefore in this Matter we desire the Favour of you to suffer us to hold our Tongues: Which tho' at this Time of Day it may sound like a very uncommon Request, yet it proceeds from the very Hearts of your Humble Servants.

By this Time the Reader perceives that more than one are engaged in the present Undertaking. Yet is there one Person, an Inhabitant of this Town of *Boston*, whom we honour as a Doctor in the Chair, or a perpetual Dictator.

The Society had design'd to present the Publick with his Effigies, but that the Limner, to whom he was presented for a Draught of his Countenance, descryed (and this he is ready to offer upon Oath) Nineteen Features in his Face, more than ever he beheld in any Humane Visage before; which so raised the Price of his Picture, that our Master himself forbid the Extravagance of coming up to it. And then besides, the Limner objected a Schism in his face, which splits it from his Forehead in a strait Line down to his Chin, in such sort, that Mr. Painter protests it is a double Face, and he'll have

Four Pounds for the Pourtraiture. However, tho' this double Face has spoilt us of a pretty Picture, yet we all rejoiced to see old *Janus* in our Company.

There is no Man in *Boston* better qualified than old *Janus* for a *Couranteer*, or if you please, an *Observator*, being a Man of such remarkable *Opticks*, as to look two ways at once.

As for his Morals, he is a chearly Christian, as the Country Phrase expresses it. A Man of good Temper, courteous Deportment, sound Judgment; a mortal Hater of Nonsense, Foppery, Formality, and endless Ceremony.

As for his Club, they aim at no greater Happiness or Honour, than the Publick be made to know, that it is the utmost of their Ambition to attend upon and do all imaginable good Offices to good Old *Janus* the Couranteer, who is and always will be the Readers humble Servant.

P. S. Gentle Readers, we design never to let a Paper pass without a Latin Motto if we can possibly pick one up, which carries a Charm in it to the Vulgar, and the learned admire the pleasure of Construing. We should have obliged the World with a Greek scrap or two, but the Printer has no Types, and therefore we intreat the candid Reader not to impute the defect to our Ignorance, for our Doctor can say all the *Greek* Letters by heart.

His Majesty's Speech to the Parliament, October 11. tho' already publish'd, may perhaps be new to many of our Country Readers; we shall therefore insert it in this Day's Paper.

His MAJESTY's most Gracious SPEECH to both Houses of Parliament, on Thursday October 11. 1722.

My Lords and Gentlemen,

I Am sorry to find my self obliged, at the Opening of this Parliament, to acquaint you, That a dangerous Conspiracy has for some time formed, and is still carrying on against my Person and Government, in Favour of a Popish Pretender.

The Discoveries I have made here, the Informations I have received from my Ministers abroad, and the Intelligences I have had from the Powers in Alliance with me, and indeed from most parts of Europe, have given me most ample and current Proofs of this wicked Design.

The Conspirators have, by their Emissaries, made the strongest Instances for Assistance from Foreign Powers, but were disappointed in their Expectations: However, confiding in their Numbers, and not discouraged by their former ill Success, they resolved once more, upon their own strength, to attempt the subversion of my Government.

To this end they provided considerable Sums of Money, engaged great Numbers of Officers from abroad, secured large Quantities of Arms and Ammunition, and thought themselves in such Readiness, that had not the Conspiracy been timely discovered, we should, without doubt, before now have seen the whole Nation, and particularly the City of London, involved in Blood and Confusion.

The Care I have taken has, by the Blessing of God, hitherto prevented the Execution of their trayterous Projects. The Troops have been incamped all this Summer; six Regiments (though very necessary for the Security of that Kingdom) have been brought over from *Ireland*; The States General have given me assurances that they would keep a considerable Body of Forces in readiness to embark on the first Notice of their being wanted here; which was all I desired 16

Major cities and towns, especially in the coastal communities, had weekly papers that carried the news of the day as well as local items. Ben Franklin's *New-England Courant* (16) had great dignity and typographic excellence. The *Boston Gazette* (18) carried Sam Adams's famous Circular Letter of Colonial grievances. The type specimen sheet (17) was issued by Benjamin Franklin Bache in Philadelphia, 1790.

A SPECIMEN

OF

PRINTING TYPES

BELONGING TO

Benjamin Franklin Bache's PRINTING OFFICE,

PHILADELPHIA.

• *French Canon Rom.*	• *French Canon Ital.*
Tandem aliq ABCDEFGJ	*Tandem aliq* *ABCDEFG*
French Canon Rom. Tandem aliqu ABCDEFGH	*French Canon Ital.* *Tandem aliquan* *ABCDEFGH*
Two Lines Double Pica Rom. TANDEM aliqua ABCDEFGHIJ	*Two Lines Double Pica Ital.* *Tandem aliquand* *ABCDJEFGHI*
Two Lines Great Primer Rom. TANDEM aliquand ABCDEFGHJKLO	*Two Lines Great Primer Ital.* *Tandem aliquando,* *ABCDEFGHK*
Two Lines Englifh Rom. TANDEM aliquando, Qu ABCDEFGHIJKLMN	*Two Lines Englifh Ital.* *Tandem aliquando, Quiri* *ABCDEFGHIKJMOS*
Two Lines Pica Rom. TANDEM aliquando, Quirites! L. Catilinam furentem audacia ABCDEFGHIJKLMNOPS	*Two Lines Pica Ital.* *Tandem aliquando, Quirites! L.* *Catilinam furentem audacia, fce-* *ABCDEFGHIJKLMNOPR*
Double Pica Rom. TANDEM aliquando, Quirites! L. Catilinam furentem audacia, fcelus anhelantem, peftem patriæ ABCDEFGHIJ KLMNOPQR	*Double Pica Ital.* *Tandem aliquando, Quirites! L.* *Catilinam furentem audacia, fce-* *lus anhelantem, peftem patriæ nef* *ABCDEFGHIJ KMNOPQR*
Double Pica Rom. TANDEM aliquando, Quirites! L. Catilinam furentem audacia, fce- lus anhelantem, peftem patriæ ne ABCDEFGHIJKLMNOPQRT	*Double Pica Ital.* *Tandem aliquando, Quirites! L.* *Catilinam furentem audacia, fcelus* *anhelantem, peftem patriæ nefarie* *ABCDEFGHIJKLMNSPQRS.*

17

BENJAMIN FRANKLIN BACHE's *SPECIMEN.*

This Indenture

Philadelphia, Pennfylvania, 1790

ABCDEFGHIKLMOP2

THE

Bofton-

AND

COUNTRY

No. 676.

Gazette,

JOURNAL.

Containing the frefheft Advices,

Foreign and Domeftic.

MONDAY, MARCH 14. 1768.

SIR,

THE House of Representatives of this Province have taken into their serious consideration, the great difficulties that accrue to themselves and their constituents, by the operation of the several acts of parliament imposing duties and taxes on the American colonies.

18

16

GEORGIA.

Sнірs or Vessels, of *any* Burthen, may be laden at the *first* Bluff, on the *North* Side of St. *Mary's River*, with LUMBER and SCANTLING for *London*, the *West-Indies* or elsewhere, with Dispatch, at reasonable Rates for Money, or in Exchange for any Kind of Merchandize. For further Particulars enquire at Mr. WRIGHT's Plantation, within a Mile of the said Bluff.

The Inlet lieth between *Cumberland* and *Amelia* Islands, is a safe Navigation, being an easy short Bar to pass over, with sufficient Depth of Water for large Ships ; it is about thirty Leagues to the Northward of *St. Augustine* Inlet. The River is bold, the Bluff in sight of *Cumberland Island*, about five Miles up the River, where Ships may in Safety load in all Seasons of the Year.

22

Advertisement.

TO be sold, a good New House, with a Kitchin, and Store-House, and a good Stable, and a Lot of Ground Containing in Front and Rear about 83 Foot in Length, about 125 Foot lying within 50 Yards of *New-York* Ferry, Landing on the high Road on *Long-Island* very convenient to keep a Shop.

Whoever Inclines to Purchase the same may apply to *Daniel Boutecou* now living on the Premises, and agree on Reasonable Terms.

23

Advertisement.

THis is to give Notice, That *Richard Noble*, living in *Wall-Street*, next Door to *Abraham Van Horn's*, Esq; in the City of *New-York*, makes White-Wash Brushes, and mends all Sorts of other Brushes, at reasonable Rates : He also gives ready Money for good Hog-Bristles, at the following Rates, *viz.* For clean'd comb'd, and five Inches in Length, one Shilling per Pound, and for uncomb'd, six Pence.

24

Franklin's influence on press notices in the Colonial newspapers was strongly felt. He conceived the idea of adding spice and interest to his pages by the introduction of small woodcut illustrations. These miniature one-inch–square cuts soon became standard equipment for all city and country newspapers, particularly for announcing ship-sailing, stagecoach, and canal-boat schedules (20, 22, 25). Another popular insertion was to advertise rewards for the apprehension of runaway servants and slaves (21).

Philadelphia, October 27. 1748.
For St. CHRISTOPHERS,
The BRIGANTINE
J A N E,
ISAAC HARDTMAN
Commander :

Now lying at Samuel M' Call junior's wharff : For freight or passage agree with Joseph Sims, or said master on board.

25

27

On the eve of the Revolution widespread dissent with restrictions imposed by the Colonial government was expressed in handbills and broadsides freely circulated in most American cities. Protest was especially vehement against importers of teas and other boycotted goods (26, 27, 28, 30), frequently calling for public meetings to discuss issues and procedure. The advertisement (31) announces the services of a professional scribe, willing to "take any side of a question, and writeth for or against, or both, if required."

The first public reading of the Declaration of Independence took place on July 8, 1776, at Philadelphia. Quoting *Harper's Weekly*, "a procession of intelligent Americans passed out of the venerable State House and, ascending a platform at the front on Walnut Street, prepared to commit an act of treason against King George, of daring self-devotion to the interests of mankind.

They had not only declared themselves free, independent; they were resolved to read publicly their declaration to their countrymen and the world. It was to be the signal to the people to rise from their bondage in Europe and America." Engraving, after a drawing by Howard Pyle which first appeared in *Harper's Weekly*, July 10, 1880.

1776-1800

A NEW NATION

THE DECLARATION of Independence gave notice to the world that the thirteen colonies had become for most purposes self-sufficient. A great number of home industries were well established by that time; communication by means of roads, ships, and the printed word was rapidly developing.

Population had increased to between two and three million, with enough concentration in larger cities and towns to support taverns and coffee houses, probably the first to use signboards. Early signs were mostly pictorial; tavern owners chose names that could be expressed pictorially: Crowing Cock, The Seven Stars, The Golden Hare, The Maypole. Tobacco shops often used the figure of a running Negro boy, an Indian with hatchet, or the figure of Sir Walter Raleigh. From the very beginning, many well-known portrait painters got their start painting signboards; Benjamin West's first commissioned painting was a picture of a hat for the Hat Tavern. Matthew Pratt, a pupil of West's and the first American portrait artist to become famous as a commercial artist, is credited with having painted the earliest authoritative likeness of Benjamin Franklin. The sign he painted for a Philadelphia tavern depicted the Federal Convention and drew great crowds trying to identify the thirty-eight figures portrayed on it.

There was a growing demand for broadsides and handbills advertising auctions, goods for sale, entertainments, and public notices. Official notices and proclamations were printed in quantity for posting at taverns and all other such places of common resort.

Colonial printing was largely utilitarian, typographically imitative of English models, and not very good. Nearly every printer, in an effort to assure a steady income beyond that received from official printing and the sale of blank forms and stationery, was moved to become a publisher of sorts. He brought out ballads of doggerel verse on any crime or scandal, calamity, or unusual event likely to catch the public interest. These were hastily put together while the news was hot and printed as broadsides to be hawked on the street for a few pence. Almanacs became a staple product of many printers. Initially simple calendars of dates and astronomical calculations, they grew to include weather forecasts, tide tables, court sessions, and much other useful information. Next to the Bible, a yearly almanac became an essential item in nearly every home.

Advertising was a vital source of income for newspapers, and merchants occasionally took a full page to list vast amounts of merchandise for sale. Long lists of books put up for auction indicate that literary customers were plentiful. Revenues from subscriptions were uncertain, and editors printed frequent appeals to delinquent subscribers. Payment was acceptable in eggs, poultry, firewood, or anything else the printer could use.

Some of the first ornamental designs were the woodcut devices, often allegorical, used in newspaper mastheads. The leading item often began with a "factotum," which was an initial enclosed in an ornamental border. The earliest illustration in an American newspaper was a woodcut of a flag in the *Boston News-Letter* of January 26, 1708. Early in 1734 this paper obtained a series of large cuts showing a post-rider, ship, angel, and dove. Most such cuts are believed to have come from England; some regularly used cuts, as for mastheads, were probably cut on metal to resist wear.

Typecast fleurons, or flower designs, first appeared in Europe during the seventeenth century, and they became characteristic adjuncts to typographic design during the following century. Besides conventionalized leaf and flower forms, English and Scottish founders sent over such small units as a crown, harp, hourglass, skull-and-cross-bones, and a variety of ingenious arabesques which could be turned and combined to produce attractive borders and large decorative patterns. These were used by Colonial printers to good effect. In newspaper advertising, small typecast pictorial trade-cuts began to appear increasingly with the approach of the nineteenth century.

Though most equipment for printing still had to be imported, some attempts at typefounding had been made, and about fifty small paper mills had been established—nearly all in Pennsylvania, New Jersey, and Delaware. The scarcity of rags for making paper was a serious handicap, and newspapers regularly printed appeals for any scraps the public could spare.

In England, it was not until 1693 that a century-old restriction against printing anywhere except in London, York, and the universities was lifted. Thus the printers in British America were technically on a par with those in the English provinces, except that they were separated from necessary supplies by the wide Atlantic. Practically all printing types first used here were of English, Dutch, and Scottish manufacture.

William Caslon (1693–1766), greatest of English typefounders, designed the type that bears his name. It has been called "the finest vehicle for the printed conveyance of English speech that the art of the punch cutter has yet devised." The first specimen sheet of *Caslon* was issued in 1734, and the new design was immediately successful. In time it became the chief type used by colonial printers. Benjamin Franklin put in a large supply, and John Dunlap used it on the first printed copy of the Declaration of Independence.

The surface of hand-made paper is uneven and requires dampening before printing in order to make a more receptive matrix for the type impression. One of *Caslon*'s virtues is that the designer seems to have made allowances for the slight thickening of the characters thus produced on soft paper. Somehow, though poorly inked and printed, even on dry paper there was something about it that still looked good. Flavorsome in the individual characters and agreeable to the eye in reading, it was the perfect type of its time, and the one most naturally associated in our minds with Colonial printing. It had a remarkable revival a few generations later, and it is still a standard face.

In spite of all its faults, eighteenth-century typography has an engaging charm that never seems to wear out. To be sure, there was seldom an attempt on the part of printers to strike out in new directions. Display lines were almost invariably centered on a vertical axis, just as in English printing; text matter was set closely and in fairly narrow columns. Excessive conservation of space must be condoned in view of chronic paper shortages, but where this was not a factor, as on title pages, the distribution of white space is often quite pleasing. Horizontal rules were a favorite device for separating areas of type; an occasional ornament or modest border added interest.

The history of American illustration begins with the woodcut portrait of the Reverend Richard Mather (1596–1669) attributed to John Foster (1648–1681), the colonies' first engraver and Boston's first printer. It was probably made about 1670. Though crude in execution, the black silhouette of the torso contrasted with the light shading of the head, hair, beard, and hands presents a powerful image of a strength much admired today. Its equal was not to appear for years to come. The self-taught Foster, though primarily a printer, cut a few other blocks, including, in 1675, a "Map of England," the first map of any kind to be printed in British America.

Like Foster, numerous colonial printers used woodcuts made by themselves or by some local "artists." Lacking large enough types, the printer sometimes cut large display words and lines in wood. Woodcuts began to appear on broadsides. One of the most interesting of these is the "Bloody Butchery" or "coffin" broadside giving an account of the Battle of Lexington, printed in Salem, Massachusetts, by Ezekiel Russell in 1775.

Across the top are forty coffin shapes in silhouette arranged in two rows, with the name of a patriot killed in the battle over each. The initial letter, all units of text, and the entire design are surrounded by heavy black borders. The use, in printing, of such borders and death emblems was quite common in those days when life was often much too short.

The covers of almanacs also received the blessings of artistic endeavor, some quite creditable, but most so crude as to be almost ludicrous. *Bickerstaff's Boston Almanac,* also printed by Ezekiel Russell in 1777, carries a portrait of John Hancock on the cover. This, and subsequent likenesses of such patriots as Gage, Washington, and Ethan Allen, are believed to have been cut by the printer. Though woefully inept, the editor proudly proclaims that "My present printer has procured for this work, at great expense, a number of plates, curiously engraved."

Of copper engravers there were a number who did quite respectable work. Among the better known were Henry Dawkins of Philadelphia, who flourished between 1753 and 1786; Paul Revere (1735–1818) and Nathaniel Hurd (1730–1777), both of Boston; and Amos Doolittle (1754–1832) of Connecticut. Copper engravers often produced historical prints, portraits, and views to be sold separately in addition to their regular commissions for engraving sheet music, trade cards, bookplates, labels, and also inserts for magazines and books. The first novel to be published in America, William Hill Brown's *The Power of Sympathy: or, The Triumph of Nature,* published in Boston, 1789, by Isaiah Thomas, had a copperplate frontispiece engraved by Samuel Hill.

Most engravers had sidelines; perhaps it would be more exact to say that engraving was an additional way of making both ends meet. Paul Revere, whose engraving of the "Boston Massacre" has become perhaps the most famous print of the Revolutionary period, was also a master silversmith. Not so well known is his work in another department. In the September 5, 1768, issue of the *Boston Gazette* he advertises that "Persons so unfortunate as to lose their Fore-Teeth by Accident . . . may have them re-placed with false ones, that look as well as the Natural, and answers the End of Speaking." John David Hechstetter, "engraver in wood, stone and ivory," announces in the June 8, 1796, issue of the *Pennsylvania Gazette* that he also "makes instruments of wood for those who have the misfortune of losing an arm or leg."

The design and printing of Colonial paper currency is a subject of great interest and variety. Some of the early notes were printed from a combination of type, typographic ornaments, and specially cut insignia and pictorial vignettes, tightly squeezed together and locked in a chase. The finished bills were numbered by hand and individually signed by an authorized person. The complicated designs were meant to discourage counterfeiting, but even in those days there were those who could make quite adequate imitations.

Franklin devised a scheme now familiar to many printmakers. By using a plaster cast of a leaf, he was able to make a metal casting of the leaf design that would last through thousands of impressions before it would wear out. As no two leaves are alike, duplication of the process was easily detectable, and for an engraver to faithfully copy every least vein in the printed leaf was impossible. Franklin kept the method a secret except from a few other currency printers, and it was used extensively on Colonial and Continental currency.

From the first, American paper money and bills of exchange were also engraved on copper. Some of these are fair imitations of the elaborate trade cards engraved in England by such masters as Hogarth, Bickham, and Bartolozzi. But these, too, could be faked, and at least one issue of Continental currency had to be withdrawn because spurious bills were of better workmanship than the genuine. During the Revolution, the British issued great quantities of counterfeit currency, most of it apparently made in British-occupied New York.

33

For the many long years of the Revolution the American people suffered untold difficulties, economic hardships, and privation. Finally the day of victory came and with it the liberation of New York from British rule. As told in *Harper's Weekly:* "On the 25th of November, 1783, was performed the last act of the war of liberation. The people of New York took possession of their metropolis. For seven years of expectation, doubt, fear, or exultation Washington had never ceased to keep his eyes fixed upon the city from which he had fled in 1776, a beaten general. He had hoped to snatch it away from the foe by some swift strategy or bold attack. He had won it at last in Virginia, and now was to enter it in peace. In the morning of the 25th a detachment of the American army had marched from Harlem as far as Grand Street; the English troops retired at their approach. The Americans took possession of the forts, lines, intrenchments, so long held by their foes." Engraved from an illustration by Howard Pyle appearing in *Harper's Weekly,* November 24, 1883, entitled "The Continental Army Marching Down the Old Bowery, New York, November 25, 1783." A selection from the Virginia newspaper (34) shows a marked improvement in typographic design and printing.

CITY - TAVERN,

Sign of the Bunch of Grapes.

THE Subfcriber informs his cuftomers, and the Public in general, that he has removed from the old houfe, where he has kept Tavern for four years paft, to his new and elegant Three-Story Brick-Houfe, fronting the Weft-end of the Market-Houfe, which was built for a Tavern, and has twenty commodious, well-finifhed Rooms in it, where he has laid in a large ftock of good old Liquors, and hopes he will be able to give fatisfaction to all who may pleafe to favour him with their cuftom.

JOHN WISE.

Alexandria, Feb. 20, 1793.   3m.

JOHN SMITH, Dancing-Mafter.

INTENDS to open a Dancing-School at the houfe of Mr. WILLIAM WILSON, Carpenter, in Water-ftreet, on *Saturday* the 20th inftant. He will teach in the moft fashionable modes at prefent: each fcholar to pay *Four Dollars* per quarter—one half to be paid on entrance, and the other half to be paid at the expiration of the quarter.

The Subfcriber has juft opened

A Houfe of Entertainment,

IN that noted and commodious dwelling, lately occupied by Mr. JOHN WISE. He has fupplied himfelf with a moft excellent Cook, who was for many years employed as fuch by the PRESIDENT OF THE UNITED STATES; has engaged two very complete Waiters; two active and fmart Oftlers; has been very particular in the choice of his Liquors, and felecting his Provifions of every kind; and as he is determined to pay the ftricteft attention to his bufinefs, he flatters himfelf, that thofe who may be pleafed to favour him with their cuftom, will not find themfelves difappointed at the ufage they fhall meet with.

Alexandria, Jan. 18, 1793.   JOHN ABERT.

MR. WILLIAMS,

PORTRAIT PAINTER.

(Late from FREDERICKSBURG.)

INTENDS to ftay a few weeks in this town. Should any Ladies or Gentlemen be defirous of having their Likenefs taken, their obliging demands will be attended to, by application being made to him at Doctor *Lang's*, in Duke-Street, where a few fpecimens of his performances may be feen.

His prices depend on the manner and ftyle of Painting—half price is expected at the firft fitting.

Alexandria, May 14, 1793.

☞ An APPRENTICE wanted by the Printer's hereof.

FOREIGN INTELLIGENCE.

NATIONAL CONVENTION OF FRANCE.

MONDAY, *January* 21.

REPORT UPON THE DEATH OF LOUIS XVI.
MADE TO THE COMMONS.

JACQUES ROUZ, (Prieft and Preacher of the Sans Culottes, one of the Commiffioners named by the Commons to affift at the execution of Louis) fpeaks:

"We come to give you an account of the miffion with which we were charged. We went to the temple where we announced to the tyrant that the hour for his execution was arrived.

"He defired fome minutes alone with his Confeffor. He wanted to give us a parcel for you; but we obferved we were only charged to conduct him to the fcaffold. He anfwered, 'that is true,' and gave the packet to our colleague. He recommended his family, and requefted that Clery, his valet de chambre, fhould be that of the Queen, and then haftily faid of his Wife. He further requefted that his old fervants at Verfailles, fhould not be forgotten. He faid to Santerre—Marchons—let us go on.— He walked through one court and got into the carriage in the fecond. The moft profound filence reigned during the whole proceffion. Nothing happened. We never loft fight of Capet, till we arrived at the Guillotine. He arrived there at ten minutes after ten—he was three minutes getting out of the carriage—he wifhed to harrangue the people—Santerre oppofed it. His head was fevered from his body. The citizens dipped their pikes and handkerchiefs in his blood!"

Santerre.—"You have heard an exact account of all that paffed. Louis wanted to fpeak of mercy to the people, but I would not let him."

Extract of a letter from Bridgetown, Barbadoes, dated the 29th inft.

"Many inhabitants of this town affembled, and had the effigy of Thomas Paine, with his "Rights of man," carried about the town; and afterwards burnt him on the parade, in the green, juft above the Cage, while the band played God fave the king." [In the true fpirit of fwine, who are known to be fo enamoured of the mire and filth of their inclofure, as frequently to lacerate the hand that lets down the fence for their deliverance.]

Feb. 15. Capt. Bligh could gain no intelligence of the mutineer Chriftian, and his accomplices, who were on board the Bounty. When they returned to Otaheite, after executing their infernal project, the natives, fufpecting fome mifchief from the non-appearance of the commander and the gentlemen with him, laid a plan to feize the veffel and crew, but a favorite female of Chriftian's betrayed the defign of her countrymen; he put to fea in the night, and the next morning the fhip was nearly out of fight.

28

A dry goods handbill of 1784 (35), neatly designed and very readable, lists an inventory of yard goods, linens, shawls, and imported oriental spices; printed locally by John Mycall. Two columns (36) selected at random from display advertisements in the *New York Daily Advertiser* in 1787. There was no attempt to segregate notices of runaway slaves from real-estate offerings, or stagecoach schedules from cabinet makers' announcements. The circus had been an accepted form of American entertainment since the country's inception. Displays of exceptional horsemanship are featured in Mr. Pool's advertisement (37), printed in New York September 21, 1786.

THOMAS BURLING,
CABINET and CHAIR-MAKER,
at the sign of the CHAIR, near the Chapel, in Beekman-street, formerly Chapel-street,

ACKNOWLEDGES the many favours received from his Friends and the Public, and would wish to inform them that he has opened a WARE-ROOM of MAHOGANY and other FURNITURE, on a more extensive plan than heretofore; and for the convenience of strangers and others, who may resort to, or settle in this city, he means to keep an assortment where they may be supplied on the shortest notice; for it must hurt the feelings of every citizen to observe the daily imposition strangers are liable to, in purchasing new furniture at these public vendues.

He served his time with Samuel Prince, a conspicuous character in his way, and esteemed one of the best workmen in this city, and as he has laid in a stock of the best Mahogany and other Wood, and means to employ the best hands, and sell his work at the lowest rate good work sells at, he flatters himself with being able to give satisfaction to his customers.

Bed-Chairs for the Sick having been much wanted in this city, said Burling has provided some to let.   tf.

To be Sold, Let, or
exchanged for Property in the City of
NEW-YORK.

A Farm at Haerlem,

ABOUT eight miles from New-York, containing about FIFTY ACRES of LAND, including salt and fresh meadow: It is pleasantly situated on the banks of the East River, and commands an extensive view of the Sound and the adjacent country. On the premises are a good commodious STONE HOUSE, a kitchen adjoining, a barn, and an orchard of several hundred trees, in the highest per...

Mr. POOL,
The first American that ever Exhibited the following FEATS OF
HORSEMANSHIP
On the Continent,

Intends Performing this Afternoon, on the Hill near the Jews Burial Ground, if the weather permits, if not, on the first fair day afterwards, except Sunday. Mr. POOL has erected a Menage, at a very confiderable expence, with feats raifed from the ground, for the convenient accommodation of thofe Ladies and Gentlemen who may pleafe to honour him with their company.

A CLOWN will entertain the Ladies and Gentlemen between the Feats.

1. MOUNTS a fingle Horfe in full fpeed, ftanding on the top of the faddle, and in that pofition carries a glafs of wine in his hand, drinks it off, and falls to his feat on the faddle.

2. Mounts a fingle Horfe in half fpeed, ftanding on the faddle, throws up an Orange, and catches it on the point of a fork.

3. Mounts two Horfes in full fpeed, ftanding on the faddles, and fires a piftol.

4. Mounts two Horfes in full fpeed, with a foot in the ftirrup of each faddle, from thence to the ground, and from thence to the tops of the faddles at the fame fpeed.

5. Mounts two Horfes in full fpeed, ftanding on the faddles, and in that pofition leaps a bar.

6. Mounts a fingle Horfe in full fpeed, fires a piftol, falls backward, with his head to the ground, hanging by his right leg, and rifes again to his feat on the faddle.

7. Mounts three Horfes in full fpeed, ftanding on the faddles, and in that pofition leaps a bar.

After which Mr. POOL will introduce a very extraordinary Horfe, who, at the word of command, will lay himfelf down and groan, apparently through extreme ficknefs and pain; after which he will rife and fit up like a lady's lap-dog, then rife to his feet and make his Manners to the Ladies and Gentlemen.

The entertainment will conclude with the noted fcene, THE TAYLOR RIDING TO BRENTFORD.

*** Every time of Performance there will be new Feats.— Mr. POOL flatters himfelf the Ladies and Gentlemen who may be pleafed to honour him with their Company, will have no reafon to go away diffatisfied;—he even hopes to merit their approbation.

The doors will be opened at Three o'Clock, and the Performance will begin at Four in the afternoon precifely.

TICKETS to be had at Mr. CHILDS's Printing-Office, near the Coffee-Houfe; Mrs. DELAMATER's, next Door to the Play-Houfe; and at the PLACE of PERFORMANCE. Price for the Firft Seats FOUR SHILLINGS—for the Second, THREE SHILLINGS.

‡‡‡ Mr. POOL befeeches the Ladies and Gentlemen who honour him with their Prefence, to bring no dogs with them to the Place of Performance.

‖‖‖ The Exhibitions will be on TUESDAYS and FRIDAYS.

New York, September 21, 1786.

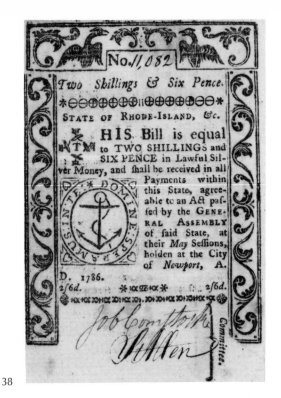

No. 11,082

Two Shillings & Six Pence.

✳⊕⊕⊕⊕⊕‖⊕⊕⊕⊕⊕✳

STATE OF RHODE-ISLAND, &c.

THIS Bill is equal to TWO SHILLINGS and SIX PENCE in Lawful Silver Money, and shall be received in all Payments within this State, agreeable to an Act passed by the GENERAL ASSEMBLY of said State, at their May Sessions, holden at the City of Newport, A. D. 1786.

2/6d. ✳☼☼✳ 2/6d.

38

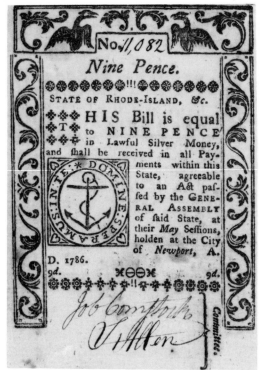

No. 11,082

Nine Pence.

✳✳✳✳✳!!!✳✳✳✳✳

STATE OF RHODE-ISLAND, &c.

THIS Bill is equal to NINE PENCE in Lawful Silver Money, and shall be received in all Payments within this State, agreeable to an Act passed by the GENERAL ASSEMBLY of said State, at their May Sessions, holden at the City of Newport, A. D. 1786.

9d. ✳☼☼✳ 9d.

39

The United STATES

No. 57543

SIX DOLLARS.

THIS Bill entitles the Bearer to receive SIX SPANISH MILLED DOLLARS, or the Value thereof in GOLD or SILVER, according to a Resolution of CONGRESS, passed at Philadelphia, May 20, 1777.

SIX DOLLARS.

40

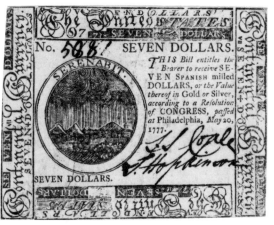

The United STATES

No. 5587

SEVEN DOLLARS.

THIS Bill entitles the Bearer to receive SEVEN SPANISH milled DOLLARS, or the Value thereof in Gold or Silver, according to a Resolution of CONGRESS, passed at Philadelphia, May 20, 1777.

SEVEN DOLLARS.

41

The United Colonies

No. 0119

EIGHT DOLLARS.

THIS Bill entitles the Bearer to receive EIGHT Spanish milled DOLLARS, or the Value thereof in Gold or Silver, according to a Resolution of CONGRESS, passed at Philadelphia, MAY 9, 1776.

EIGHT DOLLARS.

42

THE UNITED COLONIES

No. 71770 Thirty Dollars.

THIS BILL entitles the Bearer to receive THIRTY Spanish milled DOLLARS, or the Value thereof in Gold or Silver, according to a Resolution of Congress, passed at Philadelphia, JULY 22, 1776.

XXX DOLLARS.

43

45

46

47

48

49

50

51

52

53

Great difficulty and confusion resulted from the paper currency authorized by Congress in early 1776. Notes were tiny due to the scarcity of fine papers. Illiterate citizens had great trouble and had to inspect each bill carefully to determine whether it was for a dollar or some small fraction thereof, since the same design applied to many denominations. Typographic designs, before the advent of banknote engraving, utilized metal borders or wood-engraved ornaments, with printers' names often featured.

Benj. Randolph
Cabinet Maker
at the Golden Eagle in Chesnut Street
Between Third and Fourth Streets
PHILADELPHIA,
Makes all Sorts of Cabinet & Chair work
likewise Carving Gilding &c Perform'd in the Chinese
and Modern Taste

Tradesmen's cards in the latter part of the eighteenth century were styled after the decorative exemplars found in England at the time. That of Benjamin Randolph, cabinet maker (54), engraved by James Smithers, about 1770, shortly after the engraver's arrival from England, is typical of the ornate Chippendale frames of the day. Smithers was skilled as an engraver in gold and silver, made plates for currency and was accused of counterfeiting for enemy use. The card for Edward Pole, fishing-tackle maker (55), was engraved by David Tew of Philadelphia, who also made plates for paper currency. Two small cards for Paul Revere and Son (56 and 57) give but a small hint of the vast enterprise and artistic capacity of this celebrated American patriot. He also published noted political prints including that of the Bloody Massacre at Boston, 1770.

56

57

President-elect Jackson on his way to Washington, in 1828. General Andrew Jackson's journey to the capital was like a royal procession on the Old National Pike. Coaches drawn by four or six horses dashed along at a great rate of speed; the leaders of one team had their noses in the trough of the wagon ahead. Everywhere along the route "Old Hickory" was greeted by enthusiastic crowds, drawn by the magic of his military and political renown. He was frequently called upon for an impromptu speech, which the stately and courtly "Hero of New Orleans" would deliver from the driver's seat. Engraving, after a drawing by Howard Pyle, which first appeared in *Harper's Weekly* March 12, 1881.

1800-1840

GROWTH OF THE REPUBLIC

THE YEAR 1800 marks the beginning of extensive transformations in American graphic art, particularly with respect to mechanical processes. Type-foundries were established and the character of type design changed radically. Minor improvements in hand presses made printing more rapid, and stereotyping was invented. By 1814 there were some 187 paper mills in the United States, producing about 340,000 reams of paper a year.

By 1800 population stood at well over five million; in only ten years it increased another two million, accumulating a rich reservoir of graphic talent to meet the needs of business, expansion of travel, and public entertainment. Publishing began to emerge as a separate activity, principally in Boston, New York, and Philadelphia. The new nation had begun to take stock of itself and to prepare for housekeeping.

John Adams (1735–1826) had the honor of being our second President; his administration (1797–1801) presided over the opening of the new century. On June 11, 1800, the national government left Philadelphia, and the entire personnel of 126 persons moved to permanent quarters in Washington. The White House had been commenced in 1792, and John Adams, its first occupant, found it chilly and bare; Congress took several more months to appropriate $15,000 to furnish it. The Capitol building was more or less finished in 1813.

Dissemination of news about the fledgling republic was vitally important, and printers were not slow to follow the trend westward. In 1800 there were already a half-dozen newspapers west of the Alleghenies, and by 1810 there were about six hundred newspapers and periodicals in the United States. Pioneer printers somehow surmounted the horrendous problems of hauling their equipment for hundreds of miles, by water or in wagons drawn by oxen, and of procuring a steady supply of paper to print on in their ramshackle huts.

The first quarter of the nineteenth century may well be called the

"Classified Ad Period." A single issue of the *New York Gazette*. Jan. 1, 1818, contained 538 ads, occupying 25 out of 28 columns. This was not unusual for this period, and the fact that "Advertiser" appeared as part of the title of a great number of newspapers indicates the interest of publishers in this kind of revenue.

Advertising and graphic arts received potent stimulus from the expansion of travel. Some of the first users of broadsides and newspaper advertising were the many coach lines connecting important cities. But the early nineteenth century was to bring better and somewhat more comfortable modes of travel. In August, 1807, Robert Fulton's steamboat, the *Clermont,* steamed down the Hudson from Albany to New York to the astonishment of people who may never even have heard of an engine of any kind. She was described by one person who saw her pass in the night as "a monster moving on the water, defying the wind and tide, and breathing flames and smoke."

By 1811, steamboats were navigating the Mississippi, Ohio, and Allegheny rivers and the Great Lakes. The Erie Canal was opened in 1825, and the first steam locomotive appeared only six years later. All these newfangled inventions cut transportation costs sharply, not only permitting greater intercourse and distribution of goods but helping to stimulate the vogue for travel among those with the means and free time.

Perhaps the most meaningful alteration in the character of American graphic art, beginning at this time, was typographic. It was the culmination of the gradual transition from fifteenth-century roman types, derived from pen-written forms, to designs which plainly show the marks of the punch-cutter working in hard metal. About halfway in the transformation are the old-style types, of which Caslon is a good example. Though still based upon the written pen-stroke, the letters have been "cleaned up" to look more drawn than written. Further mechanical refinements appeared in the "transitional" types of the English typefounders John Baskerville (1706–1775) and William Bulmer (1746–1830). Giambattista Bodoni of Parma (1740–1813) carried the trend to its logical conclusion, creating a narrow letter with perfect vertical stress, fine hairlines and serifs, mechanically regulated curves, and decided contrast between thick and thin strokes.

The mechanical perfection of the modern face appealed to printers, and variations on it soon dominated the field, especially in book production. But the tremendous growth of advertising demanded a type which would, as it were, speak in a louder voice. It was a simple operation to exaggerate the thick strokes even more, soon leading to fat faces in which the thick strokes are sometimes nearly half as wide as the height of the letter. Though not very legible, the attention-getting blackness of these types procured wide acceptance.

The new concept of typography as a force for attracting attention in advertising had the effect of emancipating type designers from traditional restraints but caused a corresponding deterioration in taste that was to continue until the end of the century. There was no end to tinkering with the design of the alphabet to make it more elegant or attractive to the Victorian eye.

The Gothic Revival helped to resurrect the medieval gothic letters, which also suffered the indignity of being fattened to excess. These came to be known as black-letter, or Old English. What we now call gothic was originally a heavy letter without serifs, in which all strokes are of equal thickness or nearly so. American typefounders produced these not particularly attractive gothics in a bewildering variety of weights and proportions from excessively skinny to excessively black. More characteristic of nineteenth-century taste was Antique, later known popularly as Egyptian, undoubtedly in reference to current archeological discoveries along the Nile. Egyptian is a gothic letter with heavy slab serifs.

In America, several attempts to start a typefoundry had failed for lack of interest or of technical proficiency. John Baine came to Philadelphia from Edinburgh as an old man, but survived long enough to provide the type for several important Bibles and the first ten volumes of Dobson's *Encyclopedia*. He died on August 18, 1790.

It remained for Archibald Binny and James Ronaldson, also natives of Edinburgh, to establish the first permanent typefoundry in this country. Their partnership began in a rented house in Philadelphia on November 1, 1796. By 1812, they could supply sixty-eight different fonts of roman, italic, black-letter, German, Greek, Hebrew, and decorated letter. The foundry continued under various partnerships and names until its descendant firm, MacKellar, Smiths & Jordan, was absorbed by the American Type Founders Company in 1892. Binny & Ronaldson is believed to have been the first to cast a dollar sign, first used January 2, 1802, in the Philadelphia *Aurora*.

The earliest known American specimen book was issued by Binny & Ronaldson in 1809. Not a type specimen, it is a pamphlet displaying over one hundred metal ornaments, largely inspired by French sources. There are cuts of birds and beasts, ships, allegorical subjects, a zodiac figure for almanacs, numerous decorative panels, and several versions of the arms of the United States. A facsimile of this pamphlet was published in 1926. Allegorical vignettes and patriotic motifs, especially those incorporating the American eagle, were enormously popular, and foundries were to turn them out by the thousands.

Probably the most celebrated of the early typefounders were the brothers David and George Bruce of Edinburgh, who started printing books in New York in 1803. The firm became famous for its innovations in manufacture and design; many frontier printers of the Middle West and Far West were outfitted entirely by the Bruce foundry. They also introduced stereotyping into this country.

Stereotyping, a process of making papier mache matrices of entire pages of typesettings, then metal castings from the matrix, made it possible to make duplicate plates for printing. The actual type could then be returned to the typecases as good as new. The process had been perfected by the Earl of Stanhope (1753–1816), inventor of the *Stanhope* press. David Bruce managed to learn enough about it during a visit to England in 1812 for the brothers to start a stereotype foundry that same year.

The pantograph, an adjustable instrument for copying maps, plans, or other designs to scale, was widely used in the making of shadow portraits. The silhouette, named after Etienne de Silhouette (1709–1767), a French politician and amateur paper maker, had been extremely popular since 1750. Silhouetting was a lucrative pursuit; the greater availability of scissors helped to make it a hobby as well. The classic simplicity of early silhouettes was eventually corrupted with the addition of color, gilding, and fancy backgrounds. The vogue died out with the advent of photography, but silhouetting was continued by artists whose full-figure compositions are frequently found in nineteenth-century books and periodicals. The pantograph became an important tool used by wood-type manufacturers and typefounders for making graduated sizes from original patterns.

As noted earlier, general magazines failed to survive for lack of interest. However, the *Port-Folio*, Philadelphia (1801–1827), enjoyed a mild success. Strictly literary and without advertising, it was handsomely printed and occasionally presented its readers with engravings of picturesque landscapes and views for framing.

Early magazines directed to women had better luck. In New York, the *Lady's Weekly and Miscellany* (1808–1812) and the somewhat similar *Weekly Visitor and Ladies' Museum* (1817–1819) might have lasted longer if they had concentrated more on fashion than fiction.

By far the most successful was *Godey's Lady's Book* (1830–1898), published in Philadelphia by Louis Godey (1804–1878). His coeditor for forty years was Mrs. Sarah Josepha Hale (1788–1879), an aggressive feminist from Boston who, in a softer mood, wrote the famous rhyme about Mary's little lamb. It was one of the first magazines to have an elaborate wood-engraved cover. Inside were stories, poems, and articles on dressmaking and housekeeping, copiously illustrated with wood engravings and fashion plates. The name Godey has become almost synonymous with the charming steel engravings of elegant ladies dressed in the latest styles, which were the main feature of each issue. A staff of 150 ladies was regularly employed to color these plates by hand. In the late fifties, *Godey's* circulation had reached the impressive total of 150,000. Godey's most successful imitator was *Peterson's Magazine* (1842–1898). It, too, carried hand-colored fashion plates.

Graham's Magazine was also published in Philadelphia, beginning in 1840. Though its fashion plates appealed to some women, it attracted a wider readership by printing works by Poe, Bryant, Longfellow, Cooper, and other important American writers. George Graham (1813–1894) made an important contribution to magazine publishing by adding pictorial illustration as a distinctive feature. He employed the finest engravers; under exclusive contract, the painter and engraver John Sartain (1808–1897) contributed a mezzotint to each issue. Later, Sartain started a publication of his own.

More engravings appeared in books as well. Because of the high cost of foreign engravings and the security of competent engravers in this country, Collins, Perkins & Co. of New York resorted to a contest in the hope of discovering the best native talent for illustrating a new "and elegant" edition of the Bible. As a result of this scheme, according to Rollo Silver, "The *Bible,* published in 1807, is a small gallery of American engravings of the early nineteenth century."

Numerous great names of today were already established as publishers of books or magazines, or both, notably: Lippincott, 1792; Harper, 1817; Appleton, 1825; Little, Brown, 1837; Putnam, 1838; and Scribner, 1846. The American public was beginning to develop an omnivorous appetite for pictures, and parlor tables were cluttered with picture albums, elaborately decorated gift books and keepsake annuals. Publishers also profited from the growing market for entertaining literature; popular American authors prospered, and English bestsellers were pirated here almost as soon as they appeared in England. Story magazines and cheap paperbound novels flourished.

AMERICAN NAVAL VICTORIES.

WE HAVE MET THE ENEMY, AND THEY ARE OURS.

BRILLIANT NAVAL VICTORY ON LAKE ERIE.
SEPTEMBER 10, 1813.

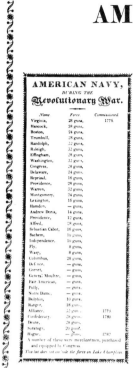

AMERICAN NAVY, DU'RING THE Revolutionary War.

Name	Force	Commissioned
Virginia,	28 guns,	1776
Hancock,	38 guns,	
Boston,	24 guns,	
Trumbull,	28 guns,	
Randolph,	32 guns,	
Raleigh,	32 guns,	
Effingham,	28 guns,	
Washington,	32 guns,	
Congress,	28 guns,	
Delaware,	24 guns,	
Reprisal,	16 guns,	
Providence,	28 guns,	
Warren,	32 guns,	
Montgomery,	24 guns,	
Lexington,	16 guns,	
Hamden,	— guns,	
Andrew Doria,	14 guns,	
Providence,	12 guns,	
Alfred,	28 guns,	
Sebastian Cabot,	16 guns,	
Sachem,	10 guns,	
Independence,	10 guns,	
Fly,	8 guns,	
Wasp,	8 guns,	
Columbus,	28 guns,	
Defence,	— guns,	
Garnet,	— guns,	
General Moultre,	— guns,	
Fair American,	— guns,	
Polly,	— guns,	
Notre Dame,	— guns,	
Dolphin,	10 guns,	
Ranger,	18 guns,	
Alliance,	32 guns,	1779
Confederacy,	28 guns,	1780
Deane,	28 guns,	
Saratoga,	20 guns,	
Hague,	— guns,	1782

A number of these were merchantmen, purchased and equipped by Congress.

This list does not include the force on Lake Champlain.

SHIPS OF THE United States' Navy, 1798, 1799.

Names	Force	Commissioned
United States,	44 guns,	1798
Constitution,	44 guns,	
Constellation,	44 guns,	
Congress,	26 guns,	1799
President,	44 guns,	
Chesapeake,	44 guns,	
Philadelphia,	44 guns,	
New-York,	36 guns,	
Essex,	32 guns,	
John Adams,	32 guns,	
Adams,	32 guns,	
George Washington,	32 guns,	1798
Boston,	32 guns,	
General Greene,	32 guns,	
Insurgent,	36 guns,	1799
Ganges,	32 guns,	1798
Portsmouth,	24 guns,	
Merrimack,	24 guns,	
Connecticut,	24 guns,	
Baltimore,	20 guns,	1799
Delaware,	20 guns,	1798
Maryland,	20 guns,	1799
Patapsco,	20 guns,	
Herald,	18 guns,	1798
Trumbull,	20 guns,	
Warren,	20 guns,	
Montezuma,	20 guns,	
Norfolk,	18 guns,	
Richmond,	18 guns,	
Augusta,	18 guns,	
Pickering,	14 guns,	
Experiment,	14 guns,	
Enterprize,	14 guns,	

And a number of smaller vessels. 1799.

In service in 1798, 24 } besides smaller vessels
1799, 50 }

Particulars of the Engagement.—On the morning of the 10th of September, the British fleet, commanded by Commodore Barclay, were discovered bearing down from Malden, for the evident purpose of attacking Commodore Perry's squadron, then at anchor in Put-in-Bay. Our squadron immediately got under way, and stood out to meet the British fleet. The line was formed at 11, and Com. Perry carried an elegant flag, which he had private ly prepared, to be hoisted at the main head of the Lawrence, on this flag was painted in characters, legible to the whole fleet, the dying words of the immortal Lawrence— "Don't give up the ship." Its effect is not to be described: the crews cheered...

Albany Argus Extra. Feb. 21.

E PLURIBUS UNUM   E PLURIBUS UNUM

An Honorable Treaty of Peace,

PROCURED BY

The valor of the   American Arms,

AND   THE

Patriotism, Persev   erance and Virtue

OF   THE

Supporters   of the War.

We received by express, at 12 o'clock this day, in connexion with the offices of the Evening Post, New-York Gazette, and Mercantile Advertiser, a copy of the Ratified Treaty, between this country and Great Britain, and hasten to lay it before the public. It was brought from Washington to Philadelphia in 14 hours, and from Philadelphia to New-York in 9, performing the whole distance from Washington to this city (240 miles) in 23 hours.—*Com. Adv.*

JAMES MADISON,
PRESIDENT OF THE UNITED STATES OF AMERICA.
To all ...

ARTICLE THE THIRD.

All prisoners of war taken on either side, as well by land as by sea, shall be restored as soon as practicable after the ratification of this treaty, and hereinafter mentioned, on their paying the debts which they may have contracted during their captivity.—The two contracting parties respectively engage to discharge in specie, the advances which may have been made by the other for the sustenance and maintenance of such prisoners.

ARTICLE THE FOURTH.

Whereas it was stipulated by the second article of the treaty of peace, of one thousand seven hundred and eighty-three, ... on his Britannic Ma... that the ...

... shall have power to adjourn to such other place as they shall think fit. The said commissioners shall have power to ascertain and determine the points above mentioned, in conformity with the provisions of the said treaty of peace of one thousand seven hundred and eighty-three, and shall cause the boundary aforesaid, from the source of the river St. Croix to the river Iroquois or Cataraguy, to be surveyed and marked according to the said provisions. The said commissioners shall make a map of the said boundary, and annex to it a declaration under their hands and seals, certifying it ... the true map of the said boundary, and ... the ... and longitude of ...

... pective reports, declarations, statements and decisions, and of their accounts, and of the journal of their proceedings, shall be delivered by them to the agents of his Britannic Majesty, and to the agents of the United States, who may be respectively appointed and authorised to manage the business on behalf of their respective governments. The commissioners shall be respectively paid in such manner as shall be agreed between the two contracting parties, such agreement being to be settled at the time of the exchange of the ratifications of the treaty. And all other expenses attending the said commissioners shall be defrayed equally by the two parties. And in the case of resignation or necessary absence, such commissioners ...

NAVAL VICTORY,

OBTAINED BY THE AMERICAN FRIGATE

CONSTITUTION,

Captain Hull—Over His Britannic Majesty's Frigate

GUERRIERE,

MOUNTING 49 GUNS—COMMANDED BY CAPTAIN DACRES.

After the War of Independence, the United States was but a pygmy among the nations of the world. Events on the high seas brought on the War of 1812 against Great Britain. The Government, with only a tiny navy at its command, fought the greatest sea power and scored impressive victories. These triumphs were proudly hailed in a number of broadsides (59 and 61) in which patriotic fervor ran high. The typographic style of these proclamations employed woodcut devices, often crudely assembled, featuring naval vessels and the omnipresent American eagle of the country's Great Seal. In the victory announcement of the *Albany Argus* dated February 21, 1815 (60), the printer chose three eagle devices from his available stock. In later years, the type-foundries cast these ever-popular emblems in giant sizes, and these were used quite frequently during the Civil War.

Ye tars of Columbia! who seek, on the main,
Redress for the wrongs which your brothers sus-
tain;
Cheer up and be merry, for Mr. John Bull
Has got a sound drubbing from brave captain
Hull,
 With his doo ra la loo.

The bold CONSTITUTION, a ship of some
fame,
Sure each jolly sailor remember's her name,
On the 19th of August, o'ertook the GUER-
RIERE,
A frigate once captured by John from Monsieur,
 With his doo ra la loo.

At five *Post Meridian* the action begun,
For she found 'twas in vain any longer to run,
So back'd her maintopsail, prepared for the fray,
As a stag when he is hunted will oft stand at bay.
 With his doo ra la loo.

Our drum beat to quarters—each jolly tar hears,
And hailed the glad signal with three hearty
cheers ;
All eager for glory, to quarters we fly,
Resolved for to conquer or bravely to die,
 With our doo ra la loo.

Proud *Dacres* commanded the enemy's ship,
Who often has sworn every Yankee to whip ;
Who always has boasted 'twould be his delight
To meet an American frigate in fight,
 With his doo ra la loo.

This boasting commander his crew now ad-
dress'd,
 Which was partly composed of AMERICANS
prest,
Says he, " my brave lads, now our wish is ful-
fill'd,
For 'tis better to capture a ship than to build,
 With a doo ra la loo.

" And *you*, who are tired of our boatswain's-
mate's whip,
And wish to return to some d——d Yankee ship ;
Twenty minutes or less of our fierce British fire,
Will gain *me* their ship and you *your* desire.
 With our doo ra la loo.

Then at it we went, in a deluge of fire,
Each party too stubborn an inch to retire,
Balls, grape-shot and langrage, promiscuously fly,
While the thunder of cannon shakes ocean and
sky.
 With a doo ra la loo.

At a quarter past six, (Yankee shot told so well)
The enemy's mizenmast tottered and fell ;
While eager to board him, the order we wait,
His foremast and mainmast both shared the same
fate,
 From our doo ra la loo.

Our cabin had now from his guns taken fire,
Yet danger but kindled our courage the higher ;
'Twas quickly extinguished, while Dacres' lee
gun,
Proclaim'd his ship ours, and the bloody fight
done,
 With a doo ra la loo.

Our prize we then boarded, all armed in a boat,
But found her so riddled, she'd scarce keep afloat ;
Fifteen of her seamen lay dead in their gore,
Where wounded and groaning lay sixty-four
more,
 With their doo ra la loo.

Our loss was but seven, who died in the cause,
Of Liberty, glory, religion, and laws ;
While the like little number will bear to their
grave,
Indisputable marks that the Yankees are brave,
 With their doo ra la loo.

Now finding our prize lay a log on the main,
A wreck that could ne'er be refitted again,
We took out the prisoners, then set her on fire,
And soon put an end to the famous *Guerriere,*
 With her doo ra la loo.

Now fill up your glasses, my lads, to the brim,
And toast noble HULL, till in toddy you swim,
Here's a health to that hero and all his ship's crew,
For a braver commander our navy ne'er knew,
 With his doo ra la loo.

61

The subscriber continues to run

the Line of Stages lately run by *George Spencer*, from Canajoharie and Palatine, by the way of Boman's Creek Meeting-House, and near the Deaf and Dumb School, to Cherry-Valley,

Twice in each Week.

62

63

JAMES BEDDO.

Proprietor of the Mail Stage, from Montgomery Ala. to Fort Mitchell.

INFORMS the Public, that his Stages are now in operation, and that he has made arrangements with Mr. Henry Crowell, and H. Knox, Proprietors of the Stage from Fort Mitchell, to Milledgeville, to keep up a regular LINE OF STAGES, twice a week, from Montgomery Ala. to Milledgeville Geo. leaving the Globe Tavern, Montgomery, every Tuesday and Friday, at 2 o'clock A. M. during the warm season; and they pledge themselves to keep good horses and carriages and to render the passengers as comfortable as the situation of the country will admit.— Each passenger will be allowed a reasonable baggage. All baggage will be at the risk of the owners Seats can be had by application at the Post Office in this place.

Montgomery, May 12. — may 19 47omo

New Line of Stages.

THE PROPRIETORS

OF THE

NEW LINE OF STAGES

CALLED THE

RICHMOND

AND

Washington Dispatch,

IN CONNECTION with the line called the *Richmond and Petersburg Dispatch*, have the pleasure to inform the Public that the line aforesaid, which formerly ran everyother day from the City of Richmond and from the City of Washington, now run from each of those Cities every day.

The above Line of Stages now being doubled, will leave the City of Richmond and the City of Washington every morning at 3 o'clock, and arrive at each of those Cities about 6 o'clock the following evening, which the Proprietors hope will gain the approbation of the Public generally.—The Stages leaving Richmond will start from the Bell Tavern, and that which runs from Washington starts from Mr. Joseph Semmes' Tavern, Georgetown; and will, on its route, call for passengers at Mr. Crawford's Tavern in the same town, and at the respective Taverns of Messrs. O'Neal, M'Leod, and M'Keowin, in the City of Washington.

The road along this new route is one of the best our country can boast. The route itself is shorter than the old one, and the fare to travellers is much cheaper, and equally as good as on the old road. These considerations it is presumed will secure to the proprietors of the *Richmond and Washington Dispatch*, as much of the public patronage as they could reasonably ask or expect. To ensure such patronage they have provided the best and most pleasant of stages, good horses, & sober, steady, and skilful drivers. Every possible attention shall be paid to baggage, but the proprietors cannot be responsible for any loss thereof.

August 17th, 1814.

64

Improved methods of transportation linking major cities and inland communities became a prime need in the early nineteenth century. American enterprise set itself to the solution: new highways were constructed and bridges built, enabling the farmer from rural "back country" areas to bring his produce to city markets. In this "Era of the Turnpike" stagecoach lines flourished. The engraving of the Concord coach in the broadsides (62 and 64) is typical of the many stage schedules posted prominently throughout the cities. The printers could purchase the needed stagecoach engravings from the foundry supply houses. These were the work of America's earliest commercial artists including Alexander Anderson, John H. Hall, William Morgan, and Abel Bowen. In lower New York in 1831, there were numerous Broadway stages, and traffic reached a level of extreme congestion, as seen in a print from *Valentine's Manual*.

For Boston.

The Sloop
RICHARD ALFRED.
Edwd. Clawson Master,
Burthen about five hundred barrels, part of her Cargo being engaged. For the remainder of Freight or Passage [having good accommodations] apply to the master on board at Smith's Wharf, or to,
HAYS and POWER.
Howard Street.

June 13.   d

For New-York,

The Sloop ROVER,
Abm. Bird, master, Jh
A regular trader, and a good substantial vessel. She will be dispatched with all possible expedition. For freight or passage apply on board, at Smith's wharf, or to   ISAIAH MANKIN,
Who offers for sale at very reduced prices, to close sales,
320 quintals Codfish, in good order, and 2000 Sugar Moulds.
may 24   d

66

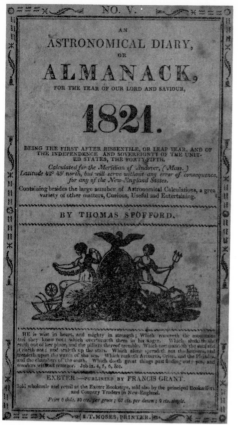

67

68

69

The continued popularity of annual farmers' almanacs (67 and 69) was due to a pattern of contents that varied only slightly from year to year: basic information on weather, climate, tides, and tried-and-true household hints, some humorous anecdotes interspersed with otherwise dry reading matter, and, later on, advertising of local merchants. The notice appearing in the *Raleigh, N.C. Register* in June of 1824 (68) offers "Ten Dollars Reward" for a runaway youth named Andrew Johnson. Similar ads were quite common in that day, except this is of special interest since it refers to a future president of the United States, who was later to face impeachment proceedings. The 1831 circus poster (70), printed shortly before Barnum began his renowned circus, shows exotic animals that could be seen in New York.

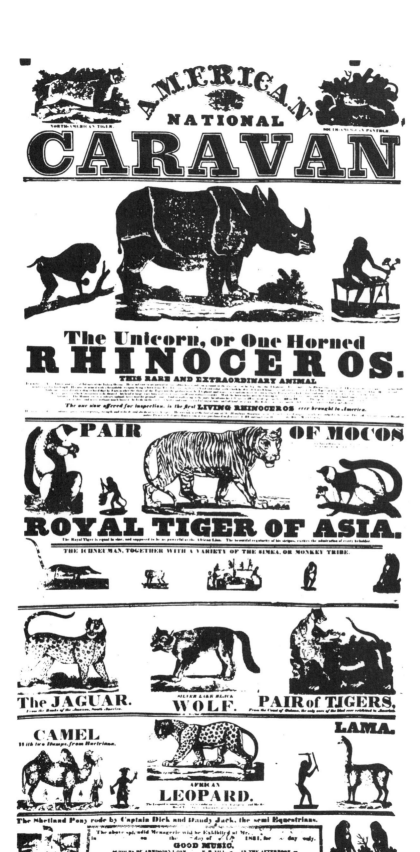

71

Slightly more than a year after the conquest of California, one of Sutter's men picked some yellow particles out of the tail-race of a sawmill belonging to his employer. The news soon spread to coast settlements, and the gold rush was on. Americans were caught in a feverish craze unlike anything the nation had ever known. In the spring of 1849 men, women, and children drove westward to begin one of the greatest migrations in the nation's history. Engraved from a drawing entitled "California Gold Diggers . . . A Scene from Actual Life at the Mines," in *Ballou's Pictorial Drawing-Room Companion,* May 3, 1856.

1840-1860

MID-CENTURY DECADES

BY MID-CENTURY, bigger and faster presses had made large-scale printing more economical and encouraged the establishment of large publishing houses and magazines with nationwide circulations. The introduction of electrotyping solved the problem of printing long runs of delicate wood engravings without breakage. Lithography was firmly established, spawning a new breed of "artists" that was to profoundly affect the direction of graphic art.

It took nearly four hundred years to make any radical changes in the ancient wooden screw hand press; after 1800, improvements appeared in quick succession. The *Ramage, Stanhope,* and *Columbian* presses introduced cast-iron construction and more efficient operation. Even better was the *Washington,* patented by Samuel Rust in 1829. After R. Hoe & Company gained control of the patent in 1835, the Hoe-Washington hand press was sold by the thousands, and many frontier newspapers were printed on it.

Isaac Adams, of East Boston, developed a press with an ingenious adaptation of hand-press principles, which could be operated by steam power. The entire complicated series of movements was automatic except the hand feeding of paper. The *Adams* press, with one feeder, could print about six times as many sheets as two men could accomplish on the old-fashioned press. Harper & Brothers had thirty-five of these *Adams* presses in their plant, upon which they printed *Harper's Magazine* as well as books.

Then, in 1814, came the astonishing news that complete copies of the *London Times* were being printed at the speed of 1,100 an hour, on presses developed by Friederich Koenig, a Saxon who had come to London in 1806 to promote his invention. Powered by steam, the press took advantage of the rapid revolution of cylinders, a completely new principle.

Stereotype molds made of papier mache were satisfactory for duplicating type forms but not sensitive enough to reproduce the fine detail of wood engravings. The galvanic battery, developed by Volta in 1800, furnished the basis for electrotyping, a method of coating a wax mold of the engraving with copper by electrolysis. The thin copper shell was then removed from the mold, backed with metal, and finally mounted on wood ready for printing.

In America, the first electrotyped plate was used in 1840, in *Mapes's Magazine,* New York. Joseph A. Adams, a wood engraver connected with *Harper's,* made extensive use of electros, and his example became an important factor in the proliferation of wood engravings in books and magazines.

The new iron presses, with improved ink distribution and greater, more even pressure, made wood engraving an attractive alternative for artists. Artistic ability was not absolutely necessary, as much of the work was copied from English models. Though largely self-taught, a number of engravers received their training from Alexander Anderson (1775–1870), generally conceded to be the father of American wood engraving.

Anderson began as a physician but abandoned medicine for engraving in 1798. As a boy he learned metal engraving from an encyclopedia, having a silversmith roll out some copper pennies to work on. He later engraved many of the vignettes displayed in Binny & Ronaldson's 1809 specimen.

More importantly, his were the first recorded American experiments in the use of a graver on the end-grain of wood as practiced by Thomas Bewick (1753–1828) in England. The fine-grained, hard wood of the box tree, when cut across the grain and polished, provided an excellent working surface for the engraver and could withstand tremendous pressure in printing from it. The circumference of this small-growing tree limited the size of the block to about five inches square, but any number of blocks could be fastened together at the back with brass nuts and bolts.

Anderson followed closely the white-line technique of Bewick and copied a great number of Bewick's cuts for American books, notably *A General History of Quadrupeds,* New York, 1804. For this he made 233 wood engravings copied in reverse from Bewick as well as over one hundred tailpieces, plus four additional animals of American origin. Anderson dominated the field through most of his long and prolific life; his work may be found in hundreds of publications of all kinds. By 1840 there were no more than twenty professional wood engravers in the United States; at the time of his death in 1870, there were about four hundred.

Cutting woodcuts with a knife is quite different from incising with a graver. Consequently, many of the earliest American wood engravings are a combination of woodcut silhouettes against completely cutaway backgrounds, with rather timidly added white-line details engraved into them. With time and practice, engravers learned to reproduce intricate line work and cross-hatching. Even textures and subtle gradations of tone came to be rendered with remarkable fidelity.

When a Bavarian playwright named Alois Senefelder (1771–1834), during the course of experiments with methods of reproducing his plays, noticed the antipathy of grease to water, he fell upon the principle which led to his invention in 1798 of lithography, or printing directly from drawings made on stone.

Originally the artist worked directly on a smooth, flat stone with fatty inks or grease pencils to form ink-receptive images. The next step was to fix the image by chemical treatment. The stone was then dampened and inked by hand for transfer of the image to paper on a hand press. As the greasy ink adhered only to the greasy image, being repelled elsewhere by the water, the result was an almost perfect facsimile, though in reverse, of the artist's drawing.

Francisco Goya (1746–1828) was possibly the first to use lithography as a medium for fine art when, in 1825, as an exile in Bordeaux, he drew four big stones of bullfights. The progress of lithography in the fine art need not be followed here, except to mention that numerous refinements in the technique were contributed by fine artists.

As a medium for commercial printing, lithography soon became a thriving industry in Germany. In England, Rudolph Ackerman, Thomas Rowlandson's publisher, made successful use of lithography and in 1819 published a complete English translation of Senefelder's now famous treatise on the subject. Modern offset and other methods of planographic printing (printing from a plane surface) are direct descendants of this simple process.

Lithography was introduced into the United States in 1828 by William and John Pendleton, plate printers and stationers in Boston, who had brought from France a Mr. Dubois, the first true litho-pressman in America. It was the Pendleton brothers, also, who employed a fifteen-year-old apprentice from Roxbury, Massachusetts, that same year. He was Nathaniel Currier. Five years later, Currier went to Philadelphia to work with M. E. D. Brown, a master lithographer. The following year he went to New York, eventually joining up with James Merritt Ives to form the famous firm of Currier and Ives.

In the use of color in printing, lithography took the lead. As early as 1835, patents were issued in Germany and France for methods of printing three colors over each other from three separate stones. In 1839, color lithography was introduced into the United States by William Sharp of Boston. Other lithographers were Major, Knapp & Co. of New York, T. Sinclair and P. S. Duval & Son in Philadelphia, and J. H. Bufford of Boston.

A common complaint among competent artists was the way their drawings were corrupted when "interpreted" by wood engravers for reproduction. They therefore welcomed the new medium, which eliminated intermediate steps in production by those less gifted. The bravura technique of the lithographic pencil was a boon to those engaged in cartooning, then as always a potent weapon in political warfare. Even Currier and Ives, the most popular printmakers of their period, issued lithographic cartoons as early as 1848; later, such prints played an important part in the election of Abraham Lincoln.

Exuberant bad taste is generally considered the hallmark of Victorian design, and it was conspicuously legitimized at the Great Exhibition of London in 1851. Colonial simplicity and Federal elegance have long been admired; to explain the lapses in taste of following decades is difficult, but we can at least point to a few negative influences in the graphic arts.

First and foremost were the commercial lithographers who were only too glad to supply advertisers and the public with whatever they wanted. The demand for novelty, overelaboration, and the exotic was satisfied abundantly and without restraint by shop-trained "artists," few of whom had had formal art education.

The addition of lettering to lithographic posters, sheet music covers, and similar jobs required the special talents of artists who understood the alphabet well enough to draw letters directly on the stone but backwards; even upside down on occasion if working on a very large stone. Quite possibly, lithography was more significant than sign writing and type design in making the art of lettering a distinct profession.

The free fancy of lithographic artists, animated by the ease with which they could work on stone, posed a serious threat to letterpress printers with more limited resources. Typefounders met the challenge by turning out a great variety of extravagantly fancy typefaces and ornaments as well as electrotypes of larger designs.

Just as offensive were some of the large wood types made in imitation of lithographic lettering. One of the first to manufacture wood type commercially was Darius Wells of New York, whose 1827 wood-type catalogue is the earliest known. The letters were cut on the end-grain with a lateral router used in combination with a pantograph. Eventually some wood types were faced with veneer or celluloid to make them more durable; after 1887 smaller sizes were stamped out by means of dies in heavy stamping machines.

The proliferation of typographic material and steady improvement in hand presses for short runs brought about a new class of craftsmen known as job printers. They specialized in such small commissions as the printing of billheads, trade cards and announcements, invitations and programs, circulars, labels, and social stationery.

Freed from the monotonous and time-consuming composition of long columns of type, job printers found pleasure in typographic innovation and seized upon any device to make their printing more attractive to prospective clients: every line in a different type, with a melange of "dingbats," fancy rules, and borders. Typefounders also supplied a fantastic variety of small units—geometric and historic designs, vines and foliage, trees, birds, animals, insects, figures, cameos, emblems, household items, and every other conceivable object—wonderfully adapted to the erection of pictorial compositions. Later, printers had flexible brass rules and specially shaped spacing material for setting type in complex curves.

Excessive ornamentation in the graphic arts was, after all, a reflection of public taste, completely uneducated aesthetically and therefore more impressed with technical virtuosity than soundness of design.

In this informative, pictorial broadside of 1840 (72), entitled "Log Cabin Anecdotes," a dozen incidents in the life of William Harrison, hero of the War of 1812, depict his military record.

He was nominated for the presidency, thus defeating the aspirations of the favored Whig party choice, Henry Clay.

A PORTFOLIO OF
MID-CENTURY ADVERTISEMENTS

Although mid-century newspapers banned prominent advertising illustrations and display typography from their columns, the new books and souvenir almanacs offered special inducements to advertisers desirous of showing their products, shopfronts, and industrial establishments. Here the ingenuity of the typographer and skill of the wood engraver and decorative designer came to the fore; typefounders met the challenge by producing miles of fancy types and ornaments. The full flavor of decorative advertising is richly communicated in the 1860 catalogue of a prominent New Haven carriage manufacturer, from which the following pages have been taken. This elaborate 226-page book is a treasure trove of mid-century design, with its 145 engravings of carriages surrounded by intricate borders, and 111 advertisements representing miscellaneous merchants, manufacturers, professions, railroads, and hotels.

73

D. W. JOHNSON & CO.,

MANUFACTURERS OF EVERY STYLE OF

CHILDREN'S

CARRIAGES,

W. H. DODD. SC.

HARTFORD, CONN.

SEND FOR CIRCULAR, GIVING FULL DESCRIPTIONS.

74

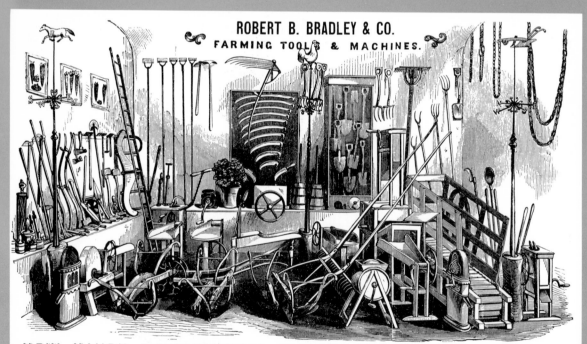

ROBERT B. BRADLEY & CO.
FARMING TOOLS & MACHINES.

NEW HAVEN AGRICULTURAL WAREHOUSE AND SEED STORE,
93 STATE STREET, NEW HAVEN, CONN.
ROBERT B. BRADLEY & CO.,

Wholesale and Retail Dealers in Agricultural Machines and Implements of the most approved kinds, and Woodenware; Field, Grass, and Garden Seeds: Fertilizers—Peruvian and Fish Guano, Phosphate of Lime, Poudrette, Bone Dust, Gypsum, &c. Also, Manufacturers of Churns, Cultivators, Corn-Shellers, Fanning Mills, Hay or Feed Cutters, Store Trucks, &c., &c.
Farmers, Planters, and Dealers, wishing our circular and price list, will be furnished by sending us their address.

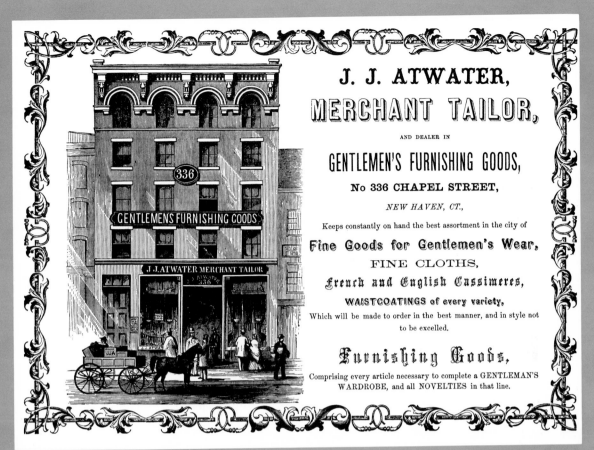

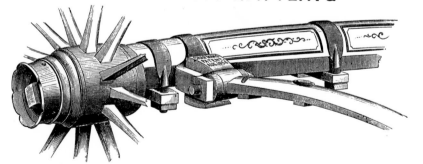

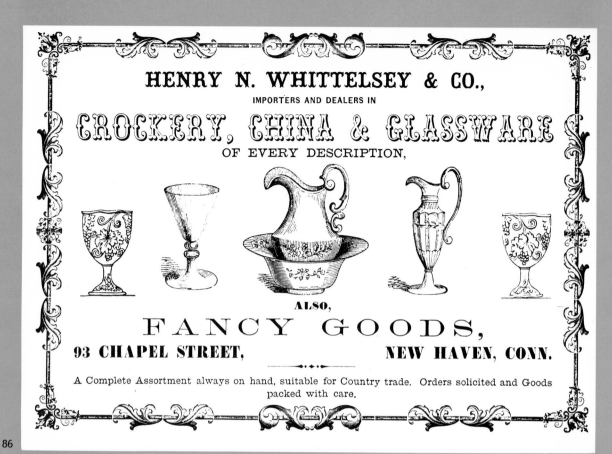

HENRY N. WHITTELSEY & CO.,

IMPORTERS AND DEALERS IN

CROCKERY, CHINA & GLASSWARE

OF EVERY DESCRIPTION,

ALSO,

FANCY GOODS,

93 CHAPEL STREET,   **NEW HAVEN, CONN.**

A Complete Assortment always on hand, suitable for Country trade. Orders solicited and Goods packed with care.

TONTINE HOTEL, NEW HAVEN, CONNECTICUT.

The subscriber has refurnished this fashionable first-class Hotel entire this Spring, remodeled the old Dining Room, added a new Ladies' Ordinary, and put in complete order his Billiard and Bath Rooms. Families can have suites of rooms at either House as low as at any first-class House in the Country. Boarders can go to and from the TONTINE to the HEAD, three times a day, by rail, and take their meals at either House, without extra charge. Having purchased and stocked a large Farm at Sachem's Head this Spring, the two Houses will be furnished with Meats, Poultry, Milk, Butter, Vegetables, and Fruit, daily, from the Farm. A Telegraph line has been put up at Sachem's Head and at the Tontine, at the Proprietor's own expense, which connects with all the lines in the United States.

MAY 23, 1860.   **H. LEE SCRANTON.**

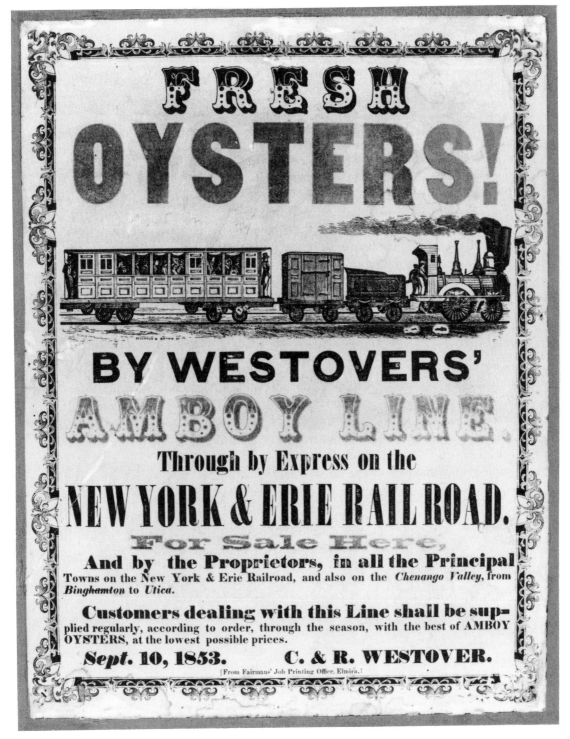

Fresh oysters had become a popular delicacy by the middle of the century, what with extended rail transportation and improved refrigeration facilities. Oyster bars and ice cream parlors sprang up in metropolitan centers as tastes became accustomed to these new delights. In this large poster (88) the printer has judiciously combined lines of gothics, decorated letters, and condensed slims, surrounded by a border of ornaments to produce an outstandingly effective broadside.

89

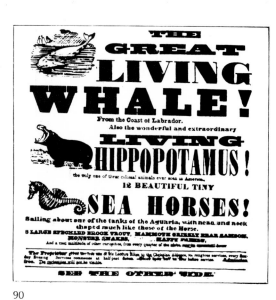

90

91

92

93

Barnum's American Museum in lower New York, where its famous owner exhibited Nature's oddities, was one of the nation's popular places of amusement. As the dean of circus and sideshow attractions, Barnum gathered human freaks from the distant corners of the globe, showing them along with rare animals seldom seen in captivity in that day. The engraving (89) shows his building before its destruction by fire in 1865, from *Gleason's Pictorial Drawing-Room Companion.* Circus broadsides (90 and 91) announced new attractions in his menagerie. Travel in the newly opened Northwest Territory (92) was advertised in the *Daily Missouri Republican,* March 9, 1840. A Kentucky dealer in imported slaves posts his prices prominently in this broadside of 1853 (93). Nathaniel Currier's announcement (94) offered "Colored Engravings for the People."

94

American Theatre
St, Philip Street.
On Monday Evening, January 17th, 1820,
Will be presented Shakespeare's celebrated
Tragedy of
HAMLET,
Prince of Denmark.:
To which will be added; Macklin's Farce of
Love a la Mode.

On Tuesday Evening, January 18,
Will be presented Goldsmith's Comedy of
She Stoops to Conquer,
Or The Mistakes of a Night.
To which will be added, by particular request,
the Opera of
ROSINA.
☞ Tickets can only be admitted on the evening for which they are purchased—this regulation is necessary to prevent counterfeits
among the door keepers.
Doors to be opened at half past 5 o'clock and
the curtain to rise at half past six o'clock
precisely.—Places for the Boxes to be taken
every day of Mr. Thos. Caldwell, from 11
o'clock till 3 at the Theatre, from whom may
be purchased a few Season Tickets.
Admittance to the Boxes $1—Gallery 75cents

The Theatre will be open every evening, Sun
days excepted.

American Theatre
St. Philip Street.
THEATRICAL NOTICE.
MR. PHILLIPS,
Late of the Orleans Theatre
Has the satisfaction of announcing to the pub-
lic, that in consequence of the arrangement
effected between himself and Mr. Caldwell,
Manager of the St. Philip street Theatre, by
which he is released from his previous engage-
ments, he will appear on the Boards of the latter
ter Theatre in the character of
ROMEO,
In Shakespear's celebrated Play of ROMEO
AND JULIET,
On Friday Evening, Jan. 21,
And that the Profits of the house on that nigh
will be appropriated to
HIS BENEFIT.
He trusts that the deference he has shewn to
public opinion, and the sacrifices which it has
cost him, will be taken into favorable consi-
deration.
Between the Play and the Farce Mrs. GRAY
will sing
"The Soldier tir'd of war's alarms."
And Mr. BOYLE will sing the favorite ballad of
"Black ey'd Susan."

American Theatre
ORLEANS-STREET.
The Manager of the American Theatre most
respectfully announces to the citizens of New
Orleans that, in obedience to the wishes of many respectable American families, and particularly with a desire, on his own part, of gratify-
ing the expectations of the French population,
he has concluded an arrangement, through the
medium of his friends, for the ORLEANS
THEATRE. The Manager will not comment
on the increased expences which he will necessarily subject himself to in the present arrangement, but merely say that, as he considers
himself the public's humble servant, he is happy in having met the wishes of those disposed
to patronise the Native drama, and his best reward will be in the assurance that he has their
approbation.
On MONDAY EVENING, Feb. 14,
Will be presented Tobin's celebrated comedy
of the
HONEY MOON.
In Act 4,
A RUSTIC DANCE,
Incidental to the Piece.
After the Play will be acted, an eccentric
comic Drama in three acts called the
THREE and DEUCE.

FRANKLIN THEATRE,
CHATHAM-SQUARE.
Benefit of the ACTORS,
Who suffered by the Burning of the Bowery Theatre.
On which occasion the following ladies and gentlemen will appear
Miss Charlotte Cushman,
Miss Waring, Mr. Ingersoll,
Mr. Woodhull, Mr. Blakeley, Mr. Gates
also, **Messrs. Cony and Blanchard,**
By permission of Mr FLYNN.
On Friday Evening, Oct. 7th, 1836,
Will be presented the two last acts of
WILLIAM TELL.
Wm. Tell,.............................Mr. Ingersoll
Gesler,..............................Mr. Woodhull

Comic Song,......"All round my hat,".....Mr. Stickney

MASTER BLANCHARD, the celebrated Contortionist will appear as the Chinese
Clown, and introduce his celebrated performances

LAST NIGHT BUT THREE OF
MR. BOOTH'S
ENGAGEMENT.
Shakspere's Tragedy.
RICHARD THIRD
Duke of Gloster   **Mr. BOOTH**
POSITIVELY LAST TIME THIS SEASON
TRESSEL, (his first appearance on any stage,) . EDWIN T. BOOTH
The Popular Farce,
SLASHER AND CRASHER.
PARTICULAR NOTICE.
A limited number of Family Slip Seats may be taken previous to the opening of the Exhi-
bition Room, which will be retained one hour after the commencement of the Performance,
at Fifty cents each seat. The Slips not so taken will remain in common with the rest of the
seats.
Monday Evening, Sept. 10, 1849.
The performance will commence with the Overture, ZAIRA, arranged by T. Comer.
After which will be acted (last time this season) the Tragedy,
RICHARD III
Or, The Battle of Bosworth Field.
(BY WILLIAM SHAKSPERE.)
DUKE OF GLOSTER, afterwards King...............Mr BOOTH
Tressel, (his first appearance on any stage)............Edwin T. Booth
King Henry 6th.........Mr Whitman | Lord Mayor............Warren

Theatrical playbills have changed little since the first public theater of Colonial times. Originally the playbill was an informative statement of fact listing the place of performance, the play's title, principal players, as well as the entire cast. This was followed with a closing date and curtain time, but the cost of tickets was rarely mentioned in these earlier announcements. In the three bills of the American Theatre of 1820, there is a quiet dignity in the type selection and design. The playbills of several decades later (98 and 99) exhibit bold lines of display type calling attention to the theater, name of the play, or featured actor. The examples of later playbills (100 and 101) show the gradual introduction of a variety of type styles and sizes approaching the flamboyant effect of the circus poster.

PARK THEATRE.

MR

Macready

AS THE

Cardinal Richelieu

Being the Last Night but ONE of his Engagement.

The Manager most respectfully announces that

MR. MACREADY

will This Evening appear for the LAST TIME, during his present' Engagement, in his original Character of the

Cardinal Richelieu!!

Boxes 1 dollar.   Pit 50 cts.   Gallery 25 cts.

TIME ALTERED

Doors open at quarter to 7   The Curtain will rise precisely at quarter past 7 o'clock.

TUESDAY EVENING OCTOBER 17. 1843.

Will be performed, the Play of

Richelieu !

OR

THE CONSPIRACY !

Cardinal Richelieu......Mr. MACREADY
Louis XIII .... Mr. Barry
Gaston, Duke of Orleans, brother of Louis XIII .... Lyne
Count de Baradas, Favorite to the King, first Gentleman of the
　　Chamber, Premier Ecuyer, &c .... Ryder
The Chevalier de Mauprat, ... Wheatley
The Sieur de Berringhen, in attendance on the King, one of the
　　Conspirators .... Andrews
Count de Clermont, ... Crocker
Father Joseph, a Capuchin, Richelieu's confident, ... Chippendale
Huguet, an officer of Richelieu's householdguard, a Spy ... Fisher
Francois, first Page to Richelieu .... Lovell
First Secretary of State .... Bridges
Second Secretary of State .... Freeland
Third Secretary of State .... Toomer
Page.. Miss Bedford
Governor of the Basile........................... Vache
Gaoler .... Povey
Gamester .... Gallot
Captain of the Archers .... King
　　Courtiers, Conspirators, Officers, Soldiers, Gamesters, &c.
Julie de Mortemar, an Orphan, Ward to Richelieu...Mrs. H. Hunt
Marion de Lorme, Mistress to Orleans, in Richelieu's pay ... Lovell

THEATRE.

On Wednesday evening, May 3,
Will be presented *Shakspeare's* celebrated TRAGEDY, in five acts, called

ROMEO & JULIET.

Romeo　-　-　Mr. Collins
Juliet　-　-　Mrs. Turner
For other characters see bills.

BETWEEN THE PLAY AND FARCE,
Songs and Recitations.
After which, a much admired musical
Farce, called
CHILDREN IN THE WOOD.
For particulars see bills.

LIBERTY HALL.

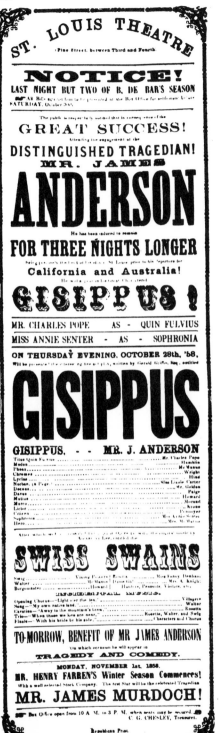

Yankee-ship sailing cards are another manifestation of a major historic episode's affecting the ephemeral graphic arts. The era of the fabulous forty-niners proved a great incentive to American ship designers, builders, and captains. Speed was uppermost and every voyage to San Francisco a race—usually only against time. The course around South America through the Straits of Magellan stretched fourteen thousand miles—a test of mettle for "Wooden ships and iron men." Donald McKay, an East Boston shipbuilder, sent out over the course one of his clippers, the *Flying Cloud*. Her record, far surpassing that of every rival, proved her one of the greatest sailing ships ever. On her maiden trip she stormed into San Francisco harbor only eighty-nine days after leaving New York, a record that has stood for all time. In the design of sailing cards the ship's name set the stage for the illustration, in an attempt to offer an unforgettable symbol so prospective passengers would choose the ship displayed. These cards were in color, more often lithographed than printed by letterpress.

NO DELAY THE EVER-POPULAR A I FIRST CLASS MYSTIC-BUILT CLIPPER SHIP **IN LOADING!**

GARIBALDI

EMERY,   Master,
IS RECEIVING HER CARGO AT PIER 20 EAST RIVER, (BURLING SLIP.)
Shippers are respectfully notified that this Favorite Clipper is again taking Cargo

FOR SAN FRANCISCO!!!

The extraordinary good order in which the "Garibaldi" delivers her cargoes is too well-known to be repeated, which, with her uniform good passages, makes her the most desirable Clipper up.

SUTTON & CO., 58 South St., corner of Wall.

The ships of this line insure at the lowest rates, and dispatched quicker than any other from New-York to San Francisco.

FOR
SANFRANCISCO
Guaranteed for June 6th.

THE A 1 EXTREME CLIPPER SHIP

SANCHO PANZA

ELIAS DAVIS, Master.

IS NOW READY FOR CARGO, AT PIER 15 E. R.

Her small capacity, unsurpassed sailing qualities, and the quick dispatch she will have, render her the most desirable vessel on the berth.

Freight can now be engaged at favorable rates, on application to

BINGHAM & REYNOLDS, 88 Wall Street.

NESBITT & CO., PRINTERS.

SMALLEST & SHARPEST CLIPPER LOADING.
Coleman's California Line
FOR SAN FRANCISCO

The A 1 Extreme Clipper Ship
SYREN

GREEN, Commander, is now rapidly Loading at PIER 11, E. R.
This beautiful little Clipper has made some of the fastest passages on record.
From SAN FRANCISCO to BOSTON, in 100 DAYS.
From NEW-YORK to SAN FRANCISCO, in 120 DAYS.
From CALCUTTA to BOSTON, in 96 DAYS,
always delivering her cargoes IN PERFECT ORDER. Shippers will find this the MOST DESIRABLE VESSEL NOW LOADING. For balance of Freight, apply to

WM. T. COLEMAN & CO., 161 Pearl Street,
Agents at San Francisco. Messrs. W. T. Coleman & Co.   Near Wall.

109

The printed book in the mid-nineteenth century was dominated by sentimental nostalgia and Victorian yearnings for the World of Long Ago. At a time when reality was moving ahead at a pace never before known in history—when railroads, steamships and other evidence of technological progress were altering the texture of humanity's thinking—the Victorians were concentrating all their artistic and literary interests on a bygone era. The design of the book, especially as represented in the over-ornate title pages, harked back to a period of rustic bowers, lacy filigree, floral and ivy-clad trellises forming a framework for titling that was readable only after careful study. Only the far away in time

111

112

and place could inspire the author and artist—
the picturesque, the foreign and above all, the
medieval. The overwhelming interest in the
gothic style, this odd vagary of fashion, could be
traced to the novels of Walter Scott and others
in the romantic movement. The gift book
blossomed as publishers brought out innumer-
able lavish, floral productions. These were heavily
illustrated, largely by lithography. For every
waxing and waning emotion, one could find in
these pretentious volumes an appropriate symbol.
Title pages were color-lithographed with the
free use of gold for embellishment (108, 110,
112, 113) and delicate steel-engraved titles (109
and 111).

113

114

115

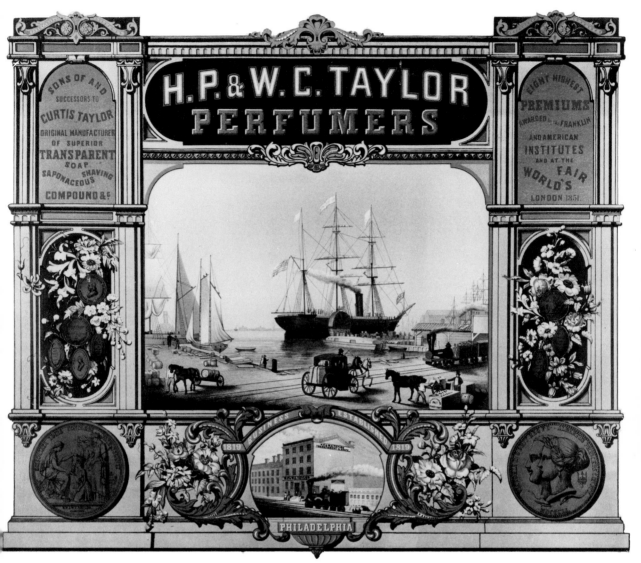

116

Tradesmen's cards of the mid-nineteenth century differ markedly in appearance from those of the post-Revolutionary era. At that time, printers followed English traditions, resulting in elaborate ornamental frames and cartouches with daintily engraved script lettering, accompanied by scrolls and flourishes. The development of lithography enabled advertisers to utilize color to make their cards most attractive and, in many instances, frameable prints. The street scene of downtown Philadelphia looking toward the Delaware River waterfront (114) shows the Louis Peck establishment in its advantageous location. It was printed in three colors around 1855 by Thomas Wagner and James McGuigan, a leading firm for the production of trade cards. In the card advertising Tarr's Marble Yard (115) a triple-arched gothic facade encloses a yard housing varied funerary monuments. This lithotint was printed by William H. Rease in Philadelphia, *ca.* 1858. One of the city's enterprising printers, Thomas Sinclair, produced the chromolithograph (116) for a noted perfumer. The vivid colors are crisply printed, with gilt medallions. The floral sprays, redolent of the product, and architectonic frame enclose a superb port scene with a paddle-wheel sailing ship loading near the Navy Yard on the Delaware. Printed *ca.* 1851.

The darkening clouds of secession and violence had been gathering for years. With the inauguration of President Lincoln the nation was filled with suppressed excitement. The future of the American people depended to a large extent upon his personal decisions and actions; and there was growing uncertainty because Lincoln was an untried man. From time to time during the winter of 1860–61 news came of the surrender of Federal forts in the South. Then came the bombardment of Fort Sumter. Shells shrieked above the gray-black water in the dim morning light, as sixty-five brave men answered the cannon fire from across the harbor. The Civil War had begun. The engraving from the *Century Magazine,* February, 1886, is entitled "Starke's Louisiana Brigade Fighting with Stones at the Embankment near the 'Deep Cut.'"

1860-1876

CIVIL WAR AND CENTENNIAL ERA

THE MOST conspicuous development in the graphic arts after mid-century was the boom in pictorial journalism created by the stirring events of the Civil War. Hardly less conspicuous was the postwar resurgence of advertising, printing, fine and graphic arts stimulated by the industrial revolution and made tangible to the entire world by the Centennial Celebration of 1876.

The first graphic products of the war were, of course, the recruitment posters printed by both sides, and the proclamations and notices posted by invading armies. Such material is of typographic interest principally because it shows the beginning of a trend toward larger and blacker type. Political posters are highly decorative and incorporate wood engravings of patriotic emblems and of candidates. During ensuing decades, political propaganda was to proliferate and include highly colorful banners, badges, buttons, and handbills.

Newspaper publishers took advantage of the newly invented telegraph to bring the latest news to their readers, stimulating sale of their papers by issuing leaflets and broadsides heralding important items to be found in the next edition. With so many men at the front, the nimble fingers of women were in great demand for setting type, as well as for many light industries.

Pictorial journalism was anticipated by *Gleason's Pictorial Drawing-Room Companion* (1851–1859) of Boston. Modeled after the *London Illustrated News,* its sixteen pages were copiously illustrated by woodcuts. The Civil War greatly accelerated the trend, providing work for hundreds of artists and engravers. Two great pictorials each had sometimes as many as a dozen artists in the field—occasionally under fire—drawing pictures for reproduction. *Harper's Weekly,* begun in 1857, had a circulation of 100,000 during the war, its pages also enlivened by the inspired cartoons of Thomas Nast (1840–1902). Preceding *Harper's* by about two years was *Frank Leslie's Illustrated Newspaper,* a more sensational sixteen-page weekly selling for ten cents. Leslie was a pioneer in getting the news out in a hurry. Leslie, like other newspaper publishers, took a shortcut in producing the large wood engravings depicting late events. The blocks for these were necessarily made of smaller blocks bolted together. After the picture had been drawn on the block, it was disassembled and the parts distributed among a force of engravers. After engraving, the blocks were bolted together again and, if time permitted, electrotyped as insurance against breakage during the long press run.

It was *Harper's,* however, that brought pictorial journalism to a kind of perfection never achieved by *Leslie's,* employing the best artists and engravers with a discrimination that has marked the entire life of the Harper publishing empire.

No doubt the most famous war artist of the time was Winslow Homer (1836–1910). As a boy, Homer was apprenticed to Bufford Lithographers, in Cambridge, Massachusetts, where he was soon put to work designing title pages for sheet music. At the outbreak of the war, Homer was hired by *Harper's* as a full-time picture correspondent, both in Washington and at the front. Homer, however, soon returned to pleasanter subjects and took up painting.

The war photos of Mathew Brady (1823–1896) were frequently copied in wood engraving for the press. Lithography and wood engraving were used in the production of war maps and books of sketches by Homer, F. S. Church, Thure de Thulstrup, Henry Sandham, Leon Moran, and many other artists whose work was to appear in magazines long after the war. Book publishers added steel engravings, mezzotints, and lithographs as inserts for books of a more permanent nature.

The conception of a newspaper as exclusively a purveyor of news and classified advertising operated toward the presentation of dreary column after dreary column of closely set small type. When newsprint became cheaper, publishers, instead of charging less for newspapers, used the savings for enlarging their pages to double previous sizes. Rivalry in the matter of size was carried to ridiculous proportions: the *New York Journal of Commerce* for a time was 35×58 inches, making a spread when open of nearly six feet! Reading one of these "blanket sheets" must have been a trial to eye and arm, to say nothing of the battalions of compositors continually setting small type day after day.

During the Civil War, advertising was shunted from the front page to the inside, where it has remained. Also, competition for readers led to the use of larger and various styles of type as column headings for important news items. Screamer headlines were still in the future.

For various reasons that now seem arbitrary, newspaper publishers resisted display advertising until well after the war. One of the reasons was technical. A new type of press, the Hoe Type Revolving Machine, first used by the Philadelphia *Public Ledger* in 1847, had an ingenious lockup device for attaching typesettings to large cylinders running in a horizontal position. An essential part of the lockup were the full-depth, wedge-shaped column rules, acting like keystones, which kept the type from falling off the cylinder. Obviously, the patented rules limited the setting of any lines wider than a column.

The fact that stereo plates could be cast on a curve solved the difficulty, and R. Hoe & Company produced a press using stereo plates in 1861. Two years later, William Bullock built for the Philadelphia *Inquirer* a cylinder press using stereo plates which could print both sides of a sheet almost simultaneously from a continuous roll. As the paper emerged from the press it was cut by serrated knives on the cylinder. Printing both sides from one feeding was called "perfecting," and the continuous sheet was known as the "web." By 1866, these presses could produce 20,000 complete papers in an hour. All of this would have been impossible had not the Fourdrinier machine been invented for turning out newsprint in endless sheets.

In spite of the greater flexibility of stereotyping, the column restrictions remained. Newspaper publishers, with a fine sense of fairness, decreed that no advertiser could overshadow another by the use of larger type. Most papers held rigidly to the old rule of "agate" type, fourteen lines of which came to a depth of slightly more than an inch. Agate is still a unit of measurement for advertising space in newspaper columns.

Some resourceful advertisers got around the agate restrictions by writing a single line or short paragraph and having it set repeatedly to fill a column. Robert Bonner's stratagem of filling an entire page of reiterated copy to promote his *New York Ledger* was the advertising sensation of 1856. Repetition of identical ads became commonplace. Another stunt was to set agate type in layers that formed pyramids or other shapes—even large letters spelling out words that straddled two or three column rules.

Display advertising with illustrations in magazines and other media finally moved newspaper publishers to follow their example, permitting clients to run ads wider than one column and in larger type. Macy, John Wanamaker, Lord & Taylor, and A. T. Stewart were some of the first to run display advertising. In 1869 Wanamaker ran the first full-page newspaper advertisement of an American store; by 1888, full-page Wanamaker ads had become commonplace.

Before lithography, black-and-white was the usual fare in books, magazines, and advertising; even chiaroscuro wood engravings were rare. Color lithography brought with it a craze for color that swept the country; the public could never get enough of it. Color suddenly blossomed out on posters and advertising ephemera of all kinds. Simultaneous with the perfecting of color lithography was an enormous demand in the market for anything printed in color that might serve a secondary purpose—or even a primary purpose: preservation in scrapbooks. Collecting colorful trifles for albums and memory books was as popular then as stamp collecting is today.

It was Louis Prang (1824–1909) who contributed most to the perfection of color printing in America, and it was he who named the process *chromolithography:* the printing in color from drawings on stone. Prang came to America from Breslau as a refugee from the German revolution of 1848. Arriving in New York in 1850, he worked in the art department of *Gleason's Pictorial.* In 1856 he went into business in Boston with Julius Mayer; Prang made the drawings on stone and his partner did the printing on a hand press. Their first job was a bouquet of roses in four colors, sold to a ladies' magazine for $250.

By 1867, Prang had the business to himself, as well as a new building housing forty presses, with seventy workmen. His early fame rested upon the quite accurate facsimiles of paintings by such artists as Winslow Homer, Eastman Johnson, Thomas Moran, and A. F. Tait.

The chromo process required a careful building up of color impressions from as many as thirty-two stones, the drawing and shading being done by workmen who were themselves artists. Prang wrote of his 13 x 10-inch chromo of Eastman Johnson's *Barefoot Boy* that it took about three months to prepare the stones, and another five to print an edition of a thousand copies. He felt that nobody could resist buying for five dollars an exact facsimile of a painting worth a thousand! He was right; he became enormously successful and world-famous.

Prang capitalized on the color craze, carrying on an extensive business in cards for Christmas, New Year's, religious purposes, and valentines, and in children's books and games. Through his highly publicized design competitions he enlisted the talents of many prominent artists and did much to bring an appreciation of art to the general public. He was especially concerned with art education for the young, establishing an educational department in his company for the production of art-instruction books. His chromo panels and promotion posters by such artists as Alphonse Mucha, Elihu Vedder, Louis Rhead, and many others were forerunners of the art-poster vogue that began in the 1880s.

The Centennial Exposition at Philadelphia, marking the first hundred years of American Independence, was a fantastic thrill to its visitors and to the millions more who read about its many wonders. During that incandescent summer of 1876 the remarkable scope of our achievements in industry and commerce, and the extent and variety of our natural resources were revealed.

Spread over the wide open spaces of Fairmount Park was a heterogeneous collection of more than 250 buildings of all sizes and styles, filled to overflowing with thirty-thousand exhibits from all parts of the Union and from fifty different nations. Though some critics found fault with the quality of the art and decoration displayed, there was universal applause for American progress in mechanics and engineering. At the west end of Machinery Hall, the Campbell Printing Press and Manufacturing Company of New York had a three-story building of its own where visitors could watch a complete newspaper being produced as well as the operation of a fully equipped job-printing plant.

The wonders of the Centennial were glowingly described in books, newspapers, and magazines; the power of print and advertising was made manifest in the sheer volume of souvenir pamphlets, printed ephemera, advertising novelties, and trade cards carried off by the public.

AN ATTACK UPON WASHINGTON ANTICIPATED!!

THE COUNTRY TO THE RESCUE!

A REGIMENT FOR SERVICE

UNDER THE FLAG of **THE UNITED STATES**

IS BEING FORMED IN JEFFERSON COUNTY.

☞ **NOW IS THE TIME TO BE ENROLLED!**

Patriotism and love of Country alike demand a ready response from every man capable of bearing arms in this trying hour, to sustain not merely the existence of the Government, but to vindicate the honor of that Flag so ruthlessly torn by traitor hands from the walls of Sumter.

RECRUITING RENDEZVOUS

Are open in the village of WATERTOWN, and at all the principal villages in the County, for the formation of Companies, or parts of Companies. ☞ Officers to be immediately elected by those enrolled.

WATERTOWN, APRIL 20, 1861. WM. C. BROWNE, Col. Comd'g 35th Regiment.

Ingalls, Brockway & Beebee, Printers, Reformer Office, Watertown.

RECRUITS WANTED!

WANTED IMMEDIATELY,

250 SAILORS

TO RECRUIT FOR THE

VIRGINIA COAST GUARD.

NOW STATIONED AT

FORTRESS MONROE.

They are to be inspected and enlisted in New-York, by order of Major General Butler, by Captain T. Bailey Myers, an Officer of his Staff, on special duty in New-York. None but those at least five feet four inches in height, and able bodied, need apply.

PAY TO DATE FROM DAY OF MUSTERING IN.

RENDEZVOUS, 360 PEARL-STREET,

OPEN FROM 10 A.M. TO 3 P.M.

D. H. BURTNETT,
Major Va. C. G. Recruiting Office.

I am authorized to inspect and enlist the above recruits, by an order from Major General Butler, dated Fortress Monroe, June 14th, 1861.

T. BAILEY MYERS,
Captain, and Acting A. Q. M.

121

War Department Washington, April 20, 1865,

$100,000 REWARD

THE MURDERER

Of our late beloved President, Abraham Lincoln,

IS STILL AT LARGE.

$50,000 REWARD

Will be paid by this Department for his apprehension, in addition to any reward offered by Municipal Authorities or State Executives.

$25,000 REWARD

Will be paid for the apprehension of JOHN H SURRATT, one of Booth's Accomplices.

$25,000 REWARD

Will be paid for the apprehension of David C. Harold, another of Booth's accomplices.

LIBERAL REWARDS will be paid for any information that shall conduce to the arrest of either of the above-named criminals, or their accomplices.

All persons harboring or secreting the said persons, or either of them, or aiding or assisting their concealment or escape, will be treated as accomplices in the murder of the President and the attempted assassination of the Secretary of State, and shall be subject to trial before a Military Commission and the punishment of DEATH.

Let the stain of innocent blood be removed from the land by the arrest and punishment of the murderers.

All good citizens are exhorted to aid public justice on this occasion. Every man should consider his own conscience charged with this solemn duty, and rest neither night nor day until it be accomplished.

EDWIN M. STANTON, Secretary of War.

DESCRIPTIONS.—BOOTH is Five Feet 7 or 8 inches high, slender build, high forehead, black hair, black eyes, and wears a heavy black moustache.

JOHN H. SURRAT is about 5 feet 9 inches. Hair rather thin and dark; eyes rather light; no beard. Would weigh 145 or 150 pounds. Complexion rather pale and clear, with color in his cheeks. Wore light clothes of fine quality, shoulders square; cheek bones rather prominent; chin narrow; ears projecting at the top; forehead rather low and square, but broad. Parts his hair on the right side; neck rather long. His lips are firmly set. A slim man.

HAROLD is a little slender, man, quite a youth, and wears a very thin moustache.

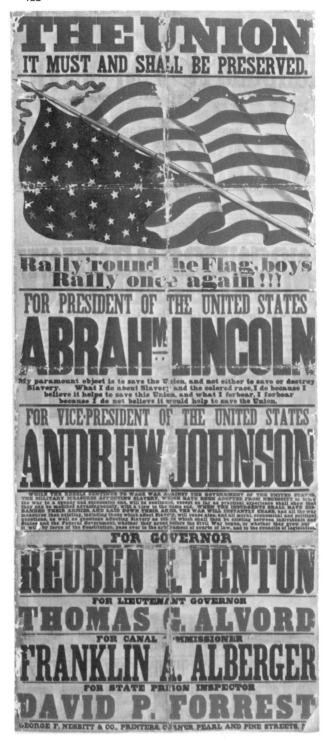

The North depended upon volunteers for its armies until the adoption of conscription in March, 1863. The scene (118) is New York City Hall Park, from an engraving in *Frank Leslie's Illustrated Newspaper,* March 19, 1864. Typical recruiting posters (119, 120) featured large wood-cut illustrations above, followed by lines of boldface display type for emphasis. An election poster (122) for Lincoln and Johnson and New York state candidates, 1861, exploits the use of boldface. The War Department issued a poster (121) announcing the reward for the apprehension of Lincoln's murderer.

GODEY'S LADY'S BOOK.

EDITED BY
MRS SARAH J. HALE,
L. A. GODEY.

VOL. LXXI.

1865.

LOUIS A. GODEY
PHILADELPHIA.

LAUDERBACH PHILA

One result of the Civil War hunger for news was the rapid proliferation of newspapers, pictorial weeklies, and periodicals. Many magazines were devoted to milady's special domain. Typical of the day, though established at a much earlier date, was *Godey's Lady's Book* (123) whose circulation was 150,000 in the late 1850s. Its wood-engraved cover is the work of J. W. Lauderbach of Philadelphia, where the magazine was published. *Peterson's Magazine* (124), a competitor of *Godey's,* reached a distribution of 140,000 in 1869.

PETERSON'S

MAGAZINE

1866

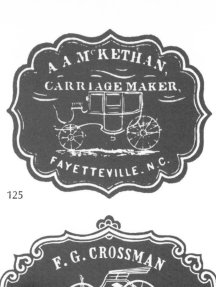

125

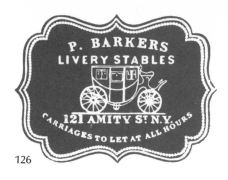

126

127

128

129

130

131

132

Of the many burgeoning industries in the country none set a livelier pace than the carriage trade, with its hundreds of coach and wagon makers, wheelwrights, lamp and leather-goods suppliers, and livery stables in every community. Carriage makers often placed a medallion on the body to indicate the builder. The printed counterparts shown on these pages, used for letterheads, invoices, and labels, form a most fascinating group of graphic devices. They were printed in attractive colors: cobalt blue, russet, vermilion, gold, and mahogany with lettering embossed in white.

WOOD, TOMLINSON & CO.

410 BROADWAY NEW YORK

133

E. C. ROBINSON

FURNITURE

WAREHOUSE

F. C. ROBINSON

69 BOWERY
N.Y.

135

CITY HOTEL,
BRATTLE
& ELM ST.
BOSTON.

136

P. H. SHAW.

& SLEIGH
MANUFACTURER.
832
BROADWAY
& 235 NORTH PEARL ST.
ALBANY, N.Y.

134

TONTINE LIVERY STABLES,
BY BARKER & RANSOM,
O. E. BARKER. REAR OF TONTINE. H. C. RANSOM.
COURT ST.
NEW HAVEN CT.

137

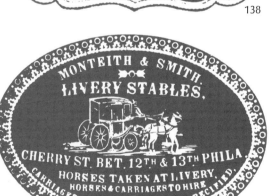

ROBT. W. HARE,
Carriage Manufacturer.
Nos. 162 & 164 Penn St. PITTSBURGH, P.A.
REPAIRING PROMPTLY DONE.

138

CITY HOTEL,
FREDERICK & SHEMWELL,
M. FREDERICK, } PROPRIETORS
P. SHEMWELL,
WILMINGTON, N.C.

139

MONTEITH & SMITH.
LIVERY STABLES,
CHERRY ST. BET. 12TH & 13TH PHILA.
HORSES TAKEN AT LIVERY,
HORSES & CARRIAGES TO HIRE
CARRIAGES READY AT ANY HOUR SPECIFIED

140

JOHN BURNS   WM. J. BURNS
BAZAAR, LIVERY & SALE STABLES,
149 Grant St. near 6th Ave. J. & W. J. BURNS, Pittsburgh, Penna.
SUCCESSORS TO
JOHN McKEOWN.
GENERAL FURNISHING UNDERTAKERS
COFFINS OF ALL KINDS, SHROUDS, CRAPE, RIBBON
GLOVES, &c. FURN. SHED AT SHORT NOTICE.
ROOMS OPEN AT ALL HOURS.

141

FORD'S THEATRE

TENTH STREET, ABOVE E.

SEASON II ....WEEK XXXI .... NIGHT 196
WHOLE NUMBER OF NIGHTS, 495.

JOHN T. FORD .... PROPRIETOR AND MANAGER
(Also of Holliday St. Theatre, Baltimore, and Academy of Music, Phil'a.)

Stage Manager...J. B. WRIGHT
Treasurer...H. CLAY FORD

Friday Evening, April 14th, 1865

BENEFIT!

—AND—

LAST NIGHT

OF MISS

LAURA KEENE

THE DISTINGUISHED MANAGERESS, AUTHORESS AND ACTRESS,

Supported by

MR. JOHN DYOTT

AND

MR. HARRY HAWK.

TOM TAYLOR'S CELEBRATED ECCENTRIC COMEDY,

As originally produced in America by Miss Keene, and performed by her upwards of

ONE THOUSAND NIGHTS,

ENTITLED

OUR AMERICAN

COUSIN

FLORENCE TRENCHARD............. MISS LAURA KEENE
(Her original character.)

Abel Murcott, Clerk to Attorney,.....................John Dyott
Asa Trenchard..Harry Hawk
Sir Edward Trenchard ....T. C. GOURLAY
Lord Dundreary ....E. A. EMERSON
Mr. Coyle, Attorney...................................J. MATTHEWS
Lieutenant Vernon, R. N. ....W. J. FERGUSON
Captain De Boots ....C. BYRNES
Binney...G. G. SPEAR
Buddicomb, a valet....................................J. H. EVANS
John Whicker, a gardener.............................J. L. DEBONAY
Rasper, a groom.
Bailiffs,...........................G. A. PARKHURST and L. JOHNSON
Mary Trenchard......................................Miss J. GOURLAY
Mrs. Mountchessington...............................Mrs. H. MUZZY
Augusta.... ....Miss H. TRUEMAN
Georgiana..Miss M. HART
Sharpe...Mrs. J. H. EVANS
Skillet ....Miss M. GOURLAY

SATURDAY EVENING, APRIL 15.

BENEFIT of Miss JENNIE GOURLAY

When will be presented BOUCICAULT'S Great Sensation Drama,

THE OCTOROON

Easter Monday, April 17, Engagement of the YOUNG AMERICAN TRAGEDIAN,

EDWIN ADAMS

FOR TWELVE NIGHTS ONLY.

BROADWAY THEATRE

Corner of Broadway and Broome Street.

Manager.........Geo. Wood | Stage Manager....T. B. Mills

MERRY CHRISTMAS

Saturday Eve'ng, December 31, 1864,

Our Greatest Comedian, Mr.

JOHN E. OWENS

In the very absurd, but irresistibly funny

Original & Ab-original Extravaganza,

Adapted by Mr. John E. Owens (exclusively for his own amusement) from the

Step-mother tongue of a half-bred Indian,

and entitled THE

LIVE INDIAN

Tom Brown...............................} Mr.
Miss Coralie Crinoline, a Mantua Maker. } J. E.
Kin-ne-no-ne-au, the Live Indian........ } Owens
Dennis O'Brien..............................Mr. Tom Owens
Lieut. Wilson...............................Mr. Fred Maeder
Mr. J. Brown................................Mr. Sol Smith, Jr.
Peter......................................Mr. Carpenter
Julia Wharton..............................Miss Nelly Johnston

New Local Scenery by Maeder.

LAST NIGHTS.

Previous to the Extravaganza, (for the 109th time,) the great Owens specialty,

the

PEOPLE'S LAWYER

Which, notwithstanding its famous and unabated success, must give place to another of Mr. Owens' great characterizations.

SOLON SHINGLE ......MR. JOHN E. OWENS
Robert Howard.............................Mr. A. H. Davenport
Hugh Winslow..............................Mr. De Groat
Mr. Otis..................................Mr. F. Maeder
John Ellsley..............................Mr. W. Fleming
Tripper...................................Mr. J. B. Bilbee
Judge of Court............................Mr. Simpson
Clerk of Court............................Mr. Beekman
Quirk.....................................Mr. Carpenter
Sheriff...................................Mr. Wilkinson
Thompson..................................Mr. Williams
John......................................Mr. G. Stanley
Timid.....................................Mr. Sol Smith, Jr
Mrs. Otis.................................Mrs. E. M. Burroughs
Grace Otis................................Miss May Preston

In preparation, Shakespeare's

Comedy of Errors

AND

Paul Pry.

No Advance in Prices.

Dress Circles and Parquette............................50 Cents
Secured Seats..............75 Cents | Orchestra Chairs.... One Dollar
Private Boxes..Six and Eight Dollars
The better to accommodate families after the vast rush to see Mr. Owens, and the eager demand for choice places, SEATS WILL BE SECURED 6 DAYS IN ADVANCE

Doors open at 7 o'clock   Performances commence at half-past 7 precisely.

Box Office open for the securing of seats from 8 A. M. til 5 P. M.

WINTER GARDEN.

Lessee and Manager..W. STUART
Stage Manager...J. G. HANLEY
Treasurer...H. J. JACKSON

GREATEST SUCCESS OF THE SEASON.

This evening, Brougham's world famous Extravaganza, **Pocahontas!** The Great Comedian **John Brougham** as **Pow-ha-tan.** The young and beautiful Comedienne, **Miss Emilie Melville** as **Pocahontas.** **J. C. Dunn** as **Capt. John Smith.**

This Evening, will be presented, with New Scenery, Costumes, and Appointments, John Brougham's Original—Ab-original—Erratic—Operatic—Semi-Civilized, and Demi-Savage Extravaganza, in 2 acts, Being a Per Version of Ye Trewe and Wonderfuile History of Ye Renowned Princess,

PO-CA-HON-TAS!

Or, Ye Gentle Savage.

Dramatis Personæ—of Ye Englishe.

Capt. John Smith, the undoubted original, vocal and instrumental, in the settlement of Virginia, in love with Po-ca-hon tas, according to this story, though somewhat at variance with his story...J. C. DUNN
Lieut. Thomas Brace, second in command a hitherto neglected genius, whose claims on posterity are now, for the first time, acknowledged as his right......................J. MILOT
William Brown, sometimes called Bill, another of the same sort...............DUN BROWN
Mynheer Rolff, the real husband of Pocahontas, but dramatically divorced, contrary to all law and fact..C. M. WALCOT, Jr
Benjamin Brace........... | Splicers of main braces, shiverers of timbers | ...MR. GO-AHEAD
John Junk................ | general dealers in single combats, double | ...MR. COME-UP
Henry Halyard........... | hornpipes, and altogether amazingly naughty- | ...MR. SPARR
William Bunting......... | cal people. | ...MR. MAST HEAD

Of Ye Savages.

H. R. H. POW-HA-TAN I, King of the Tuscaroras—a crotchety Monarch—in fact a Semi-Brave...MR. JOHN BROUGHAM
Right Hon. Quash u Jaw, Speaker of the Savage House of Lords—straightener of unpleasant kinks, an oiler of troubled waters, unraveller of knotty points, adjuster of pugnacious difficulties, and Grand Eye Parliamentary Factotum and Fugleman....................T. J. LEIGH
O po dil-doc, one of the Aboriginal F. F. V.'s, an indignant dignitary....................J. DUELL
Col-o-gog, another warm headed and hearted son of Old Virginia, the untiring.......MR. W. B. ANDREWS
Ri-jin-go Sergeant at-Arms, a friend to swear by....................................L. CARLAND
Ip-pah-kke...J. BULL
Sas-sa-prll............. | Medical Men of the Saultz | ....A. FISH
Kod-liv-royl........... | and Senna-ca Tribes | ....A. GEW
Katomel

H. R. H. PRINCESS PO-CA-HON-TAS, the Beautiful and very properly undutiful Daughter of King Powhatan, married according to the ridiculous dictum of actual circumstances to Master Rolff, but the author flatters himself much more advantageously disposed of in the acting edition.......................................MISS EMILIE MELVILLE
Poo-tee pet......... | Interesting offshoots from the aristocratic stock, | ...MISS FANNY STOCQUELER
Dl-mun-dl.......... | superior to the first families of Virginia, embody- | ...MISS DUNN
Wee- he-ven-da..... | ing the rigid principles of the Tuscorora Fashion- | ...MISS MARY CARR
Kros-as-kan be..... | able Finishing School. | ....MISS MOORE

Music Incidental to the Piece.

Solo and Chorus—"O, how about it!"......................Pow-ha-tan and Chorus
Air—"Wid a Dandoon,"...Pow-ha-tan
Solo and Chorus—"Come Forward"..................Pow-ha tas and Indians
Grand Scena—"As you are, oh "...................John Smith and Indian
Varioso—"Where the Idlers".....................................Po-ca-hon tas
Quintet and Chorus—"Fill now the Flowing Glass"..........Pow-ha-tan, Po-ca-hon-tas and Smith
Grand Finale—"Effectuoso—Furioso—E Conglomeroso".......Po-ca-hon-tas and Indians
Come, let us now like Watch Dogs Bark.................John Smith and Indians
Operatic Duet.....................................John Smith and Po-ca-hon tas
Characteristic Concerted Piece—" Now for a Jolly encounter"...Po-ca-hon-ta, John Smith, Pow-ha tas
Grand Finale—" And now we have done our duty".........John Smith, Pow-ha-tan, Po-ca-hon-tas and Chorus

Between the Comedy and the Extravaganza the Orchestra will perform

THE SCOTIA POLKA,

Composed by **JOHN BROUGHAM**, and dedicated to Captain JUDKINS.
The orchestral arrangement by ROBERT STOEPEL.

Part 1.—The Departure—" Warning Bell"—Steam up—Paddle Wheel Accompaniment—Dinner—" Life on the Ocean Wave.
Part 2.—A Dark Day—Trouble Ahead—The Chief Engineer puts on his "foul weather shirt"—The "Duck" in a Storm—The Winds Whistle, so does the "Bos'n"—The Thunder Speaks, so does the Commodore.
Part 3.—" All's Well"—Glass rises—Sea falls—Passengers Jolly—An eight day trip—The " Arrival" and the "Welcome Home."

144

OLYMPIC THEATRE

Broadway, Near Bleecker Street.

James E. Hayes.........Lessee and Manager. Asa Cushman.........Stage Director
Dan Symons.........Business Manager. F. Danse.........Leader of the Orchestra

FIRST WEEK.

THIS AND EVERY EVENING
AND
WEDNESDAY AND SATURDAY MATINEES

Geo. L. Fox

WILL APPEAR AS

HAMLET

In T. C. DE LEON'S New Version of Shakespeare's Masterpiece of that name.

With Entire New Scenery........by...................James E. Hayes, T. Johnson and Assistants
Costumes........................by......................Madame Trimble
Properties......................by......................Wm. Henry
Machinery.......................by......................James Tate and Assistants

This Entirely NEW VERSION, written by T. C. DE LEON, Esq., of Mobile, expressly for MR. GEO. L. FOX, under whose immediate supervision the piece is produced, assisted by Mr. J. J. Wallace, the Author's representative, and holder of copyright.

Fourth Appearance at this Theatre of
MISS BELLE HOWITT,
MISS LAURA QUEEN,
MISS FANNY QUEEN,
MISS JULIA QUEEN,
MISS BLANCHE BRADSHAW,
MRS. BRADSHAW,

MR. BEN MAGINLEY, and **Mr. LESTER CAVENDISH,** (from across the water),

And the **FULL STRENGTH** of the **COMPANY** in the CAST.

Claudius, King of Denmark..................................Mr. Ben Maginley
Hamlet (H. D.), son of the former King and nephew of the present King.....Mr. Geo. L. Fox
Polonius, Lord Chamberlain...................................Mr. Lester Cavendish
Horatio, friend to Hamlet.....................................Mrs. Blanche Bradshaw
Laertes, Son of Polonius.....................................Mrs. Marie Longmore
Rosencrantz........... | Courtiers | ....Mr. J. M. Charles
Guildenstern.......... | | ....Mr. Geo. F. Ketchum
Osric, a Courtier...Miss Fanny Queen
Priest...Mr. Connolly
Marcellus, an officer...Mr. G. A. Bean
Bernardo, an Officer..Miss Laura Queen
Ghost of Hamlet's Father.....................................Mrs. Edw. Wright
First Actor...Mr. H. C. Cunningham
Second Actor..Mr. S. Wright
Actress..Mr. Asa Cushman
Gravedigger...Miss Julia Queen
Gertruda, Queen of Denmark and the mother of Hamlet..........Mrs. Bradshaw
Ophelia, Daughter of Polonius................................Miss Belle Howitt

☞ Spectators are requested to remain contentedly seated till the close of this laughter provoking Travestie, as the noise made in departing by the impatient few mark the pleasure of those anxiously awaiting the Funny Climax of this highly enjoyable performance.

NOTICE.—There will be no change of time, either at the **Evening** or **Matinee** performances, the former commencing at 8, and the latter at 2 in the Afternoon.

MATINEES every Wednesday and Saturday at 2.

SECOND HAMLET MATINEE
WITH
MR. GEO. L. FOX
SATURDAY, FEBRUARY 19, 1870.

For the better Accommodation of the Public, the Box Sheet will be open at the Box Office of the Theatre, and at the Ticket Office, 114 Broadway,

TWO WEEKS IN ADVANCE.

RATES OF ADMISSION :

Orchestra and Balcony Chairs...............$1.00 | Dress Circle and Parquette............75 Cents
Reserved Seats in Dress Circle.............$1.50 | Family Circle.........................50 Cents
Children under 10.........................(in Matinee only)........................25 Cents
Balcony Chairs............................(in Matinee occasions)..................Begins at 2 o'Clock
Doors open at 7½ | Begins at 8 o'Clock. Terminates at 10:45. Doors open for Matinee at 1. Begins at 2 o'Clock

SEATS SECURED SIX DAYS IN ADVANCE FOR EITHER MATINEE OR EVENING PERFORMANCES.

Undoubtedly the most renowned of theatrical playbills is that of Laura Keene's performance in *Our American Cousin* (142), at Ford's Theatre in Washington the night of President Lincoln's assassination. It is typical of hundreds of printed programmes, with eight different display types clearly indicating the who, where, what, and when of the advertised performance. John E. Owens, a noted comic performer, achieved great success in many American cities before he carried his Yankee roles to the London Strand. The playbill announcing his appearance (143) exhibits a recognizable typographic style common to bills of the period. Most of these theatrical playbills are the work of only a few specialized printers. The extravaganza called *Po-Ca-Hon-Tas* (144) had an unusually large cast, so the playbill does not emphasize special features. In the playbill for *Hamlet* (145) a script face provides a slight variant from customary top billing.

146

In 1876 the Centennial Exhibition commemo-
rated the nation's first century of progress with
impressive displays of industrial, agricultural,
and social advances. Some ten million visitors
were awed by this most lavish exhibition of all
time. They traveled by train, bus, bicycle, or on
foot from distant corners of the land. Most exciting was the giant Corliss Engine in Machinery
Hall, a 700-ton monster that towered several
stories above their heads. Other machines
included powerful newspaper presses, steam
engines, looms, agricultural machines, and the
telephone. The exhibition left little doubt that
America had forged ahead of its European
friends, and visitors went home imbued with
patriotic pride in America's great achievements.
A mass of published volumes described the many
exhibits and opened up vast vistas of glorious
days ahead, stimulating the graphic arts and
advertising as no other single event in our
history had done. From an engraving after a
drawing by Schell and Hogan in *Harper's
Weekly,* June 3, 1876.

In the 1870s ephemeral printing utilized the
greatest possible variety of decorative and display
faces to attain effects then in vogue. To keep
abreast of the times the printer had to stock new
faces being offered by the typefoundries, in
addition to countless families of assorted type
ornaments and embellishments. Cards, tickets,
letterheads, invoices, and related forms ran the
gamut of elaborate ornamentation (147, 148). A
firm of wood engravers demonstrates their con-
summate skills (149), not with type ornaments
but with delicately designed scrolls rendered in
wood.

Inauguration
OF
CLIFTON HALL,

Monday, February 14th, 1870.

Cards of Admission must be exhibited at the Door, and are not Transferable.

147

148

LITTLE MIAMI, COL. & XENIA, and MARIETTA & CINCINNATI R. R.

RAILROAD PASS.

COMPLIMENTARY.

No.............. Loveland, O.............................1870.

Permission is hereby given to THE BEARER, and all his friends, to travel from any Station on the **L. M., C. & X. and M. & C. R. R.** or from any part of Clermont, Warren, and Hamilton Counties, on foot, to the OLD-ESTABLISHED NEW YORK STORE of

M. KAPLAN,

to see the bargains he is now offering in all kinds of goods for Ladies' and Gentlemen's wear.

NOT TRANSFERABLE.

GOOD UNTIL USED.

149

Stillman & Adams
Designers,
WOOD ENGRAVERS
AND
Printers.
51 WEST FOURTH ST., CINCINNATI.

150

151

152

153

154

Labels, cards, tickets, and assorted oddments of printed ephemera gave the compositor a golden opportunity to indulge in wild extravagance and virtuosity, and yet in the result there was an underlying unity of expression, typographically speaking. The romanticism and mysticism of the Victorian era, so dominant an influence in art, architecture, and literature, also was apparent

PHŒNIX

TIME-TRIED. FIRE-TESTED.

INSURANCE COMPANY, HARTFORD.

Assets:

$1,681,148.86

Losses Paid:

$5,000,000.00

Chamber of Commerce Agency—A. S. Reeves, Agt.

155

A. HIRSCH,

LATE OF

HIRSCH & SCALLAN,

The Boot Maker

161 RACE STREET,

2d door above 4th,

CINCINNATI.

Particular attention paid TO "STYLE."

156

157

W. S. BROWN.   P. CLEARY.

W. S. BROWN & CO.

Steamboat Agents,

No. 20 Public Landing,

CINCINNATI.

158

GEORGE MELDRUM,

Window Glass, Paints, Brushes, Painters' Materials, etc. etc.

No. 23 West Fourth Street,

Cincinnati, 187

on the printed page. Letter forms in this era were twisted and distorted, compressed and squeezed into slim shapes, and again extended into fat versions, sometimes outlined, at other times thrown into three-dimensional variants. Throughout these pained mutations, there was the strong influence of the Gothic revival as developed abroad and imitated here at home.

89

TILE & CASTOR,
FASHIONABLE HATTERS.
FURS,
MISSES' BONNETS,
GENTLEMEN'S HEAD-PIECES,
&c. &c.

159

MRS. BONNETLOVE,
MILLINER.

PARISIAN STYLE: AMERICAN TASTE:
EXQUISITE CONTOUR.

160

POPAWAY & BANG,
GUNSMITHS.
APPROVED SHOOTING IRONS
AND ALL
SPORTING ACCESSORIES.

161

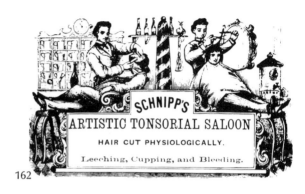

SCHNIPP'S
ARTISTIC TONSORIAL SALOON
HAIR CUT PHYSIOLOGICALLY.
Leeching, Cupping, and Bleeding.

162

MORTAR BLUEPILL,
Graduate of the College of Pharmacy.
Practical Pharmaceutist.

PRESCRIPTIONS CAREFULLY COMPOUNDED.

163

PUMPKINVILLE STORE !
FRESH GOODS FROM THE EAST !
GEWGAWS FOR GIRLS !
TOMFOOLERIES FOR BOYS !
FANCIES FOR WOMEN !
Substantials for Men !

TZADDI SHARPEYE,
MAIN STREET.

164

SUNBEAM,
PHOTOGRAPHER,
123 Skyhigh Building,
HELIOTROPOLIS.

Likenesses twice as natural
as Life.

165

T. POTT,
DEALER IN
AMBROSIAL
TEAS,
SWEETMEATS,
EDIBLE BIRDSNESTS,
&c. &c.

166

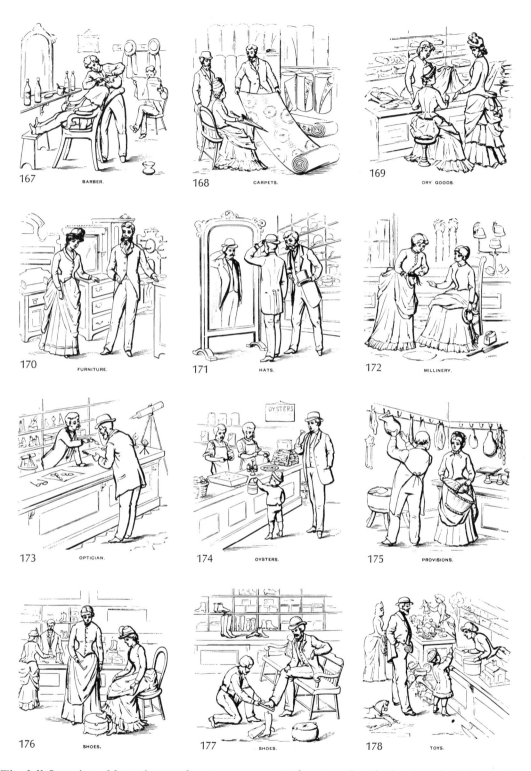

167   BARBER.

168   CARPETS.

169   DRY GOODS.

170   FURNITURE.

171   HATS.

172   MILLINERY.

173   OPTICIAN.

174   OYSTERS.

175   PROVISIONS.

176   SHOES.

177   SHOES.

178   TOYS.

The full flowering of late nineteenth-century advertising and printed matter was in no small measure dictated by the unrestrained outpourings of the typefoundries. There was as yet no established advertising art group, except for a few wood engravers in the larger cities. Thus the typefoundry offered hundreds of well-designed stock cuts so that the butcher, the baker, or the candlestick maker could illustrate his trade on cards, letterheads, and invoices. The business cuts (159–166) exhibit the bits of whimsical humor some foundries used to enliven their notices. Quite a different style was developed in other series (167–178).

179

The decades following the Centennial witnessed a tremendous growth in all areas of the nation's economy. It resulted from widespread technological progress, the extension of railroad lines and spurs in all directions, the westward trek in pursuance of our "manifest destiny." Thousands made fortunes in land and stock speculation and spent freely in an opulent society noted for luxuries and extravagances, new sports and divertissements. No wonder that Mark Twain coined the descriptive phrase "The Gilded Age," aimed primarily at lampooning swindlers, spendthrifts, and politicians who in their free-spending habits forgot the nation's poor, its strikes and depressions. It was a period of great contrasts when achievements and agonies went hand-in-hand. The illustration, entitled "Lawn-Tennis Tournament for the Championship of New Jersey," is from an engraving after a drawing by W. P. Snyder, appearing in *Harper's Weekly*, July 10, 1886.

1876-1900

THE GILDED AGE

THE POWERFUL impetus given to American graphic arts by the 1876 Centennial Exhibition was soon apparent in the nation. Advertising began to grow in all directions. Billposting firms were established; professional sign painters covered barns, fences—even the sides of cliffs—with huge advertisements. Riders in streetcars saw rows of placards mounted above the windows. Business streets were so cluttered with hanging signs and banners that city authorities were obliged to regulate their size and number.

Chromolithography in advertising also flourished. The majority of larger advertising items have disappeared; enough of the smaller pieces, saved because they were "pretty," are found among scrapbooks of social ephemera and trade cards to testify to the tremendous breadth of the industry.

Trade cards were the largest category of advertising ephemera before book matches were invented, and the first to be mass produced. Averaging 3×5 inches, they were lithographed in huge quantities, often in series like the later chewing-gum and tobacco cards.

Whether the kittens, or children, or pretty ladies depicted on them had any connection with the products advertised was apparently immaterial in most cases. Fancy lettering was discreetly worked into the backgrounds, and merchants had a wide choice of unspecific pictorial designs with a small space for imprinting. For professional and personal use there were stock calling cards with sprays of flowers.

The unsanitary distribution of food products in bulk was on the wane; more and more items were put in packages. Packaging saved the grocer's time in weighing and wrapping; the consumer was pleased with its cleanliness; the manufacturer was able to identify his goods and thwart substitution (not genuine without this signature), and to display his package or trademark in advertising. The packaging of cereals changed the breakfast menus of the nation; bottling and labeling created an enormous market for soft-drink manufacturers.

The medical profession was full of quacks, and after the Civil War patent medicine manufacturers flourished. It was a time of miraculous pads and electric belts and all kinds of tonics, elixirs, and pills "guaranteed" to cure anything that ailed you, make you young and beautiful or successful in love. Medical Almanacs, "doctor" books, sex and marriage guides offered sure-fire products which could be ordered by mail. Patent-medicine promotion displayed all the hoopla of the circus in traveling medicine shows, complete with hootchy-kootchy dancers and painted Indians. The gullible public bought and bought until rescued from false claims by the Pure Food and Drug Act of 1906.

National advertising required the services of agents who compiled lists of available space in magazines and newspapers all over the country. Some agents bought large blocks of advertising space and resold it to advertisers at a large profit. When publishers caught on to this dodge, advertising agencies had to be satisfied with a set commission, plus any charges for preparing the advertisements for their clients. Manufacturers could also buy space in preprinted inserts syndicated to thousands of small newspapers throughout the nation.

Magazines were slow to accept advertising, considered beneath their dignity. However, the first issue of *Scribner's Magazine*, 1887, carried some thirty pages of ads ranging in size from two agate lines to full pages. All were lumped together in one section, a practice that was to be characteristic of magazine advertising for a long time. (The *National Geographic* and a few other magazines still do it.) Advertisers got their first concession from publishers with the inclusion of cartoons among the ads. Now, of course, consumers are lured into the ad sections by runovers from stories and articles.

Photography completely revolutionized pictorial reproduction in the seventies and eighties. Innovations came in quick succession. First, the camera's lens made it possible to photograph an artist's drawing to a different size, and in reverse, directly onto the specially prepared surface of a woodblock, which was then given to a wood engraver. This process had hardly been perfected when it was found that an image drawn in clear black lines and transferred photographically to copper or zinc could be treated so that the work formerly done by the hand engraver could be done quickly and accurately by the corrosive action of acid. Photographic reproduction of linework greatly stimulated the practice of pen draftsmanship, so brilliantly typified by such masters as Edwin Austin Abbey (1852–1911) and Charles Dana Gibson (1867–1944).

Inevitably the photoengraving process was perfected for the reproduction of continuous tones as well by photographing the artwork through a fine screen which broke up the image into acid-resistant dots, graduating in size from almost imperceptibly tiny in the lightest areas to large and over-lapping in the darkest areas. Greater contrasts were achieved by hand engraving and burnishing.

Just as inevitable was the extension of the halftone technique to full-color reproduction by means of camera filters which separated the image into four printing plates, one for black and one for each primary color—red, yellow, and blue—a considerable improvement over initial successes with three-color halftones made in 1892.

The gradual transition from hand work to photographic reproduction is evident in magazines of the period displaying wood engravings, line drawings, halftones, and color reproductions side by side; also in the work of such an artist as Howard Pyle (1853–1911), whose career bridged the gap from hand to camera.

Second-class mailing privileges, granted by the Postal Act of 1879, permitted lower subscription rates; lower costs of reproduction encouraged greater use of pictorial material, including photographs. Both contributed to the growth of magazine publishing.

A high birth rate and heavy immigration between 1870 and 1900 brought the population up to 75 million, providing greater circulations for already established magazines. Important new ones appeared, among them: *McCall's*, 1870; *Popular Science*, 1872; *Woman's Home Companion*, 1873; *Ladies' Home Journal* (as *Ladies' Journal*), 1883; *Good Housekeeping*, 1885; *Cosmopolitan*, 1886; *Collier's*, 1888; and *Vogue*, 1892.

Etching played no part in American graphic arts except for some minor excursions into the etched reproduction of paintings and the production of a few bookplates and other ephemera. Steel engravers, however, found ample scope in the printing of bank notes and stock certificates. The overly ornate styles in these items had much to do with the excessive ornamentation displayed in other kinds of printing; typefounders issued many alphabets and designs imitative of bank-note engraving.

Before 1861, all paper currency was issued from private banks; much of it was deliberately worthless or became so as the issuing banks went broke. Regulation became imperative at the start of the Civil War, and Congress began the process by authorizing notes to be backed by the United States. These notes were printed in green ink on the reverse to differentiate them from State Bank Notes and were promptly called "greenbacks."

Efforts to baffle counterfeiters led to the invention of ingenious machines. The geometric lathe produced complicated networks of fine lines crossing each other and curving back again with mathematical precision. Parallel lines used for shading letters and backgrounds were made with a ruling machine. The same sort of machine was used for medallions. Using a coin or medal as a pattern, the machine drew unbroken parallel lines from edge to edge, copying every undulation of the relief with unerring exactness. Pictorial vignettes were engraved by hand, but wherever possible, sky, water, and backgrounds were made by machine.

By the middle of the century, American bank-note engravers were the best in the world, doing much of the work for foreign governments as well. Frequent use of semi-draped females in vignettes was encouraged by the growing public acceptance of chaste nudes in salon art and the wide publicity given to the *Greek Slave,* sculptured in 1843 by Hiram Powers (1805–1873). One of the best artists and engravers to popularize such subjects was Asher B. Durand (1796–1886). Durand, not daring to ask even his wife to pose in the nude, paid a large sum for John Vanderlyn's *Ariadne,* first exhibited at the Paris Salon of 1812, so that he could study the naked female form conveniently and without embarrassment.

Probably the most beautiful and elaborate pieces of paper currency ever produced by the Bureau of Engraving and Printing were the three notes in the "Educational Series" of 1896. However, there was carping criticism of the dollar bill, and the main figure on the five-dollar note was considered "too naked." A new series replaced it in 1899. Since then our paper money has lost much of its aesthetic appeal, though undeniably it has other charm for those who possess it.

After 1880, the Industrial Revolution was in full swing, showering the public with such luxuries and conveniences as the camera, the typewriter, the fountain pen, the telephone, the cash register, the bicycle. People had more time for entertainment, and the frolics of the "Gay Nineties" extended into nights made bright by incandescent lamps.

In Washington, President Cleveland pushed a button at the White House that turned on all the electric lights at Chicago's great Columbian Exposition of 1893. Of the 20 to 30 million visitors that summer, a great number spent much of their time and money in the carnival atmosphere of the mile-long "Midway Plaisance," made forever famous by "Little Egypt," the Oriental belly dancer.

The Fair was a white city, seven miles in circumference, full of white buildings in the neoclassic style that Louis Sullivan predicted would corrupt American architecture for another fifty years. He was right. But art and design were heading in a new direction. Victorian fustian was no longer fashionable; proponents of the Arts and Crafts Movement were in favor of simplicity and functionalism. The new aesthetic was understood to mean "art for Art's sake" and included peacock feathers and swirling fabrics, the pleasures of eye and intellect rather than sentimentality. It was the period of Art Nouveau and the Art Poster.

Art posters and the craze for collecting them were probably the most interesting manifestation of the new aesthetics. The posters of Chéret, Lautrec, and other French masters were well known and admired for their refreshing simplicity. Understandably, the more literary magazines—*Harper's, Century, Lippincott's,* and *Scribner's*—were the first to use art posters for covers and newsstand display. Some of the finest of these were done by Louis Rhead (1857–1926), Edward Penfield (1866–1925), and Maxfield Parrish (1870–1966).

Bicycle manufacturers were also early users of posters for advertising. With the arrival of the safety bike in the late eighties, cycling became the most popular sport for young and old; by 1896 it was estimated that there were over a hundred thousand bicycle fans in the United States. For a long time, bicycle manufacturers dominated the advertising pages of magazines as well.

Will Bradley (1868–1962) was a prolific poster artist and one of the first to introduce Art Nouveau to our shores. His bicycle posters were a great success. Essentially a line artist, he nevertheless knew how to make effective use of solid areas of color, contrasting them with delicate penwork reminiscent of Aubrey Beardsley and heavier decorations inspired by the Kelmscott books of William Morris.

Bradley was also one of the first to demonstrate the great potential of graphic design to the business world. In *Bradley: His Book,* an art and literary magazine he published and printed at his own Wayside Press in Springfield, Massachusetts in 1896 and 1897, he insisted upon designing every advertisement. These were redesigned for each issue; in fact it was Bradley who introduced the custom for magazines to change their covers regularly.

182

The circus posters (180–182) are representative of commercial lithography which had, by the seventies and eighties, grown to a sizeable industry, located mainly in the midwest. Typical was the Strobridge Company in Cincinnati, which produced enormous quantities of theatrical and circus posters for firms throughout the country. It employed a large staff and in the first half of 1881 turned out over 1,500 new designs. The artists, many first- and second-generation German-Americans, were proud of their craft but worked, for the most part, anonymously. Large, detailed compositions were necessary to portray the busy circus scene. The posters were rendered in a "nice and smooth" technique using highly finished crayon drawing directly on stone, with stipple effects to produce realism. Garish color schemes and bold lettering were dictated by the billboard's need to attract attention at a distance and at the same time to convey the bizarre and the spectacular aspect of the big tent.

185

183

186

184

187

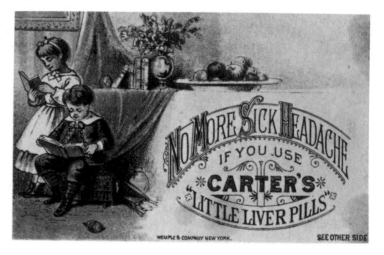

These miniature chromolithographed trade cards produced and printed by the millions swept the country during the "card craze" of the eighties and nineties. They advertised everything from soothing syrup to corn cures, baby's nipples to breast developers, mowing machines to lawn mowers. An outgrowth of Currier and Ives' engravings the pictures were eagerly sought, collected, and mounted into albums to grace the parlor table.

A PORTFOLIO OF
EARLY POSTERS

The Art Poster was essentially of European origin, stimulated by examples designed by such prominent artists as Steinlen, Gavarni, Lautrec, Mucha, and especially Jules Chéret, whose lively posters were collected—even peeled from walls and hoardings. The craze for Art Posters soon spread to this country, creating a fertile field for the best efforts of American artists. Bicycle manufacturers and magazines were the first to make use of Art Posters, issuing many of them in manageable size calculated to encourage collectors to buy and preserve them. Though the earliest posters show plainly the French influence, a distinctly native style soon developed in the work of such masters as Bradley, Penfield, Parrish, and Rhead.

188

The growing interest in posters was stimulated by several sources after the seed had first been planted abroad. The monthly magazine in the 1890s broke away from the staid, standardized covers, changing them for each issue. This opened the field for many illustrators, among them young Maxfield Parrish who, in 1895, won a national poster contest. His *Scribner's* and *Century* covers (189, 190) were lithographed in 1897.

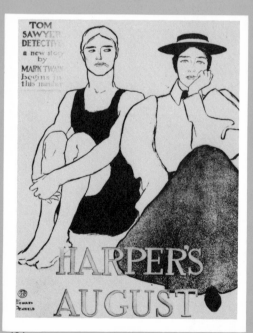

193   194

As a young illustrator and art director employed by *Harper's,* Edward Penfield was commissioned to design a different poster each month (191–194), a practice that continued for six years. These posters were avidly collected, not only in America but in Paris, London, and Berlin where the postermania had thousands of devotees. His Orient Cycles poster (195) was one of several for this prominent bicycle maker at the height of the wheel craze.

195

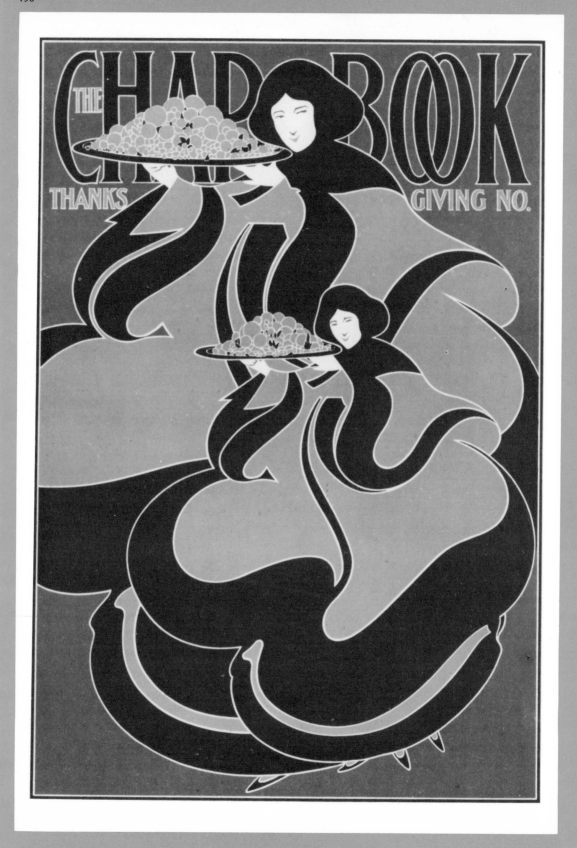

Many consider Will Bradley to be the dean of early poster designers. Certainly his work, like that of his confrere Edward Penfield, was much in evidence and collected by a coterie of ardent admirers. Born in Boston in 1868, he moved to Chicago where, in March, 1894, he began drawing posters for Stone and Kimball, publishers of the successful miniature magazine, the *Chap Book* (196). The poster for Tom Hall's novel *When Hearts Are Trump* (197) was executed in December, 1894.

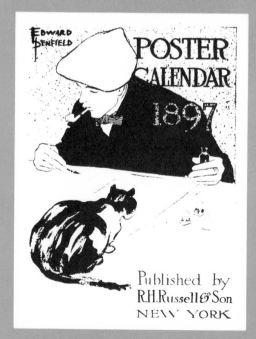

202

203

204

The poster fever enjoyed a brief yet meteoric rise between 1893 and 1896, during which time the American public collected whatever was printed, and sometimes, as was the fad in Paris, stripped them from the billboards as soon as they were posted. It all started with Penfield's series for *Harper's Magazine*. By 1896, as reported in *"Posters in Miniature"*: "The absence of any new designs showing originality has seen its best days." However, while the poster craze subsided, many new issues continued to appear. Will Bradley's offerings (198, 199), both dated 1896, were everywhere in evidence. Penfield's *Poster Calendar* (200) proved very popular and was immediately sold out as the edition was very limited. Louis Fancher did the *Scribner's* poster (201) in 1907. Louis J. Rhead, who had a one-man show of his posters in New York, did the Lundborg Perfume designs (202, 203), and Ethel Reed the song-sheet cover (204). All three were done in 1895.

The Health Jolting Chair

COPYRIGHT.

The most important Health Mechanism ever produced

A Practical Household Substitute for the Saddle-Horse.

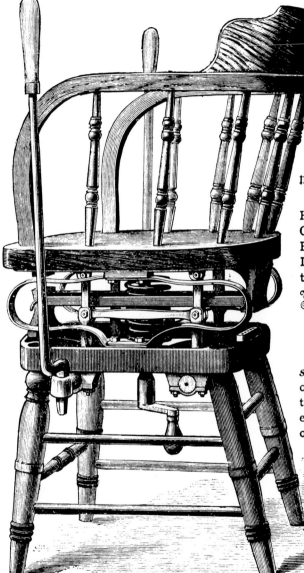

It affords a PERFECT means of giving EFFICIENT exercise to the ESSENTIALLY IMPORTANT NUTRITIVE ORGANS OF THE BODY in the most DIRECT, CONVENIENT, COMFORTABLE, and INEXPENSIVE manner.

Suitable for all ages and for most physical conditions.

INDISPENSABLE TO THE HEALTH AND HAPPINESS OF MILLIONS OF HUMAN BEINGS WHO MAY BE LIVING SEDENTARY LIVES through choice or necessity.

It preserves Health, cures Disease, and prolongs Life.

An *ingenious, rational, scientific, mechanical* means of overcoming those impediments to the taking of proper exercise, erected by the artificial methods of modern society.

For certain classes of invalids a veritable Treasure-Trove.

A CONSERVATOR of NERVOUS ENERGY.

No dwelling-house is completely furnished without The Health Jolting Chair.

206

Magazines carried a variety of advertising, but none more blatant in their claims than those for cure-all remedies offered by the health and drug industry: "electric belts" to restore manhood, glandular aids to stimulate sex, and mechanical chairs touted as a "practical household substitute for the saddle-horse"—literature sent on request failed to mention the spring-winding needed for a few moments of the shakes.

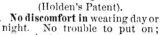

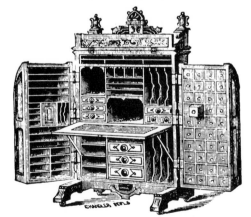
207

These small advertisements are typical of the sales efforts for the new gadgets and appliances of the day. The tricycle, the telephone, the magic lantern, and the garter were popular subjects for sales promotion. The Wooton Cabinet, "the desk of the age," today is a highly prized item.

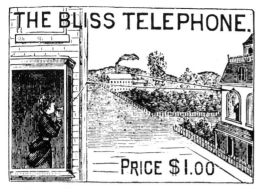
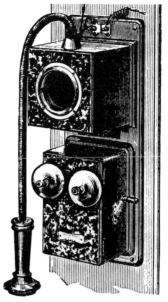

208

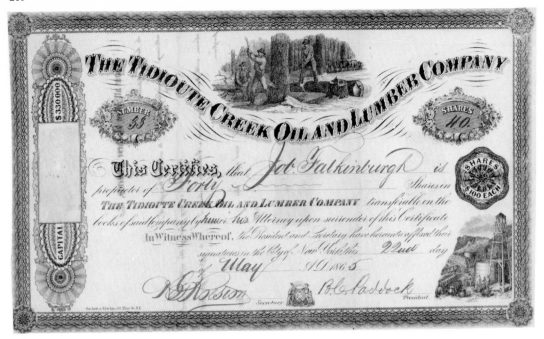

Stock certificates, bonds, and banknotes, in their design and production, are a field separate and distinct from letterpress printing and lithography. They exhibit the masterly steel-engraving techniques in which American mechanical methods proved vastly superior to anything being done in Europe. Elaborate scroll borders, delicate script lettering, and detailed vignettes all combine to make the counterfeiter's task more difficult.

211

212

213

More than any other single artist of the turn-of-the-century epoch, Charles Dana Gibson captured the suave elegance of an elite society and its unique nouveau riche attitudes. Unmistakably upper-crust, very often aloof and slightly bored, his ideal American women and their equally handsome male companions are pictured in drawing rooms, salons, at the beach, or attending the horse races. Gibson's success with his illustrated books and magazine pages inspired a host of imitators. His "Gibson girl" has become a symbol to the social historians of the more affluent phase of young twentieth-century America. Pen and ink drawing by Charles Dana Gibson from his book *The Weaker Sex* published in 1903.

1900-1920

A WORLD POWER EMERGES

THE PERFECTION of photographic reproduction, the invention of machines for setting type, and superior printing methods laid the foundation for a tremendous surge in the graphic arts of our century. Early twentieth-century advertising in periodicals was generally without distinction, typographically uninteresting, and seldom supported by competent commercial artists. Wood engraving remained the favorite medium for small cuts in advertising and for picturing the merchandise offered in the bulky catalogues of Montgomery Ward, Sears Roebuck, Butler Brothers, and a dozen others.

We must therefore look to the editorial content of magazines for the first signs of improvement. Prosperous magazines paid handsome fees for artwork and attracted a great number of fine illustrators. C. D. Gibson received a thousand dollars each for his drawings. His "Gibson Girl," once described as "fashioned for masculine adoration, but absolutely unresponsive," became world-famous. Magazines brightened their covers with colorful paintings made to order, a new one for each issue. The vogue for "pretty girl" covers began with such facile and prolific artists as Harrison Fisher (1875–1934) and Howard Chandler Christy (1873–1952), whose paintings, along with those of many other illustrators, were reprinted for framing.

The effectiveness of attractive pictures in selling magazines was not lost on national advertisers and their agencies; advertising illustration later became a lucrative profession participated in by most of the artists first known for their magazine work.

The idea of setting type by machine was a will-o'-the-wisp that had brought many inventors and their backers to grief. Mark Twain is said to have sunk three million dollars into a typesetting machine invented by James W. Paige. The machine had 18,000 parts, which probably accounts for its failure in a test conducted by the Chicago *Herald* in 1894. Twain had casually turned down an offer to invest in the Mergenthaler Linotype, to the eternal sorrow of his ghost.

Ottmar Mergenthaler's Linotype Machine was a brilliant invention which could cast a single line or slug of type from brass matrices brought into position by means of a keyboard. It was first used by the New York *Tribune* in 1886 and soon became standard equipment in newspaper plants.

Another American invention was the Monotype machine of Tolbert Lanston, the first patent for which was granted in 1887. Its name stems from the fact that it casts separate pieces of type instead of complete slugs. From a keyboard the operator perforates a paper ribbon, and the perforations in turn drive the casting machine by means of compressed air. As on the Linotype, the matrices are automatically returned to the mat chambers after casting. The Monotype is the favorite instrument for quality printers and for bookwork.

The Ludlow system, suggested by W. I. Ludlow and perfected by A. Reade in 1906, is a method of casting slugs of larger types. Each line is cast from brass matrices set by hand and locked in a Ludlow composing stick. After casting and proofing each line, the matrices are immediately returned to the cases by hand. Ludlow is especially useful for setting headlines and advertising display.

The rapid expansion of the typefounding industry had posed some problems. One was the antiquated custom of expressing type sizes by about twenty names such as Brevier, Bourgeois, and Paragon—their ambiquity compounded by conflicting ideas among founders as to their exact measurements. This was righted in 1886 by adoption of the American point system. A point was fixed at .01387 inch, and a pica as measuring 12 points. Roughly, 72 points, or six picas, equal one inch.

The second problem proved to be economically disastrous. Demand for foundry type diminished drastically as more and more large printing plants discontinued hand setting in favor of machine composition. There were at least twenty-five important typefounders in 1871, but increasing competition for business resulted in failures and mergers, with the American Typefounders Company on top as a virtual monopoly before 1900. Their 1912 catalogue of type specimens and printing equipment was an impressive and hefty 10-pound book of over thirteen hundred pages. Gone were the outlandish faces of previous years, replaced by a number of more traditional designs. The punch-cutting machine developed by Linn Boyd Benton from the old principle of the pantograph made it possible to mechanically cut an entire range of type sizes from a single set of patterns. One of the first faces cut on this machine was *Cheltenham* (ATF, 1902), designed by Bertram Grosvenor Goodhue. Though Goodhue was an architect and knew nothing much about lettering, his design unaccountably enjoyed unprecedented popularity for many years. Another successful—and still popular—

face was *Century,* originally made about 1890 by Benton for *Century* Magazine. Most new text faces, including some gothics, were adapted to machine composition.

One of the most influential printers of his time was Theodore Low DeVinne (1828–1914), a scholar and graphic arts historian as well. His writings did much to shape the course of printing, especially with respect to its standing as a fine craft. It was for him that the Warren Paper Company made the first coated paper for the better printing of wood engravings and halftones. His work as a printer of books and magazines is technically impressive but typographically stodgy by our standards; he was soon eclipsed by younger craftsmen with fresh ideas imported from England.

The Kelmscott Press books of William Morris (1834–1896), appearing during the ferment of the Arts and Crafts Movement, were undoubtedly the most potent inspiration for the new generation of graphic artists. Morris created his own decorations and had type cast from his own designs, but he employed expert workmen to do the typography and printing. He was largely responsible for the resurrection of the private press as an instrument of printing as a fine art. A confirmed medievalist, his meticulously crafted books were actually a printer's version of the medieval manuscript style. Their densely packed black type and heavily decorated woodcut initials and borders were in marked contrast to the arid conceptions and spindly types of his contemporaries.

The Kelmscott style was widely imitated, and there was a rash of elaborate borders and decorative initials in all kinds of printing and advertising. More importantly, Morris's conception of a book as a unified whole was gradually understood and became a principle of good design now taken for granted.

The early work of such master printers and typographic designers as D. B. Updike, John Henry Nash, Bruce Rogers, Frederic Goudy, and Will Bradley plainly show the influence of William Morris. But the Morris ideal was also misinterpreted and vulgarized by Elbert Hubbard (1856–1915), a cultural poseur whose Roycroft books, atrocious parodies of the Kelmscott style, had a ready sale at the time.

The revival of interest in book design paralleled the general awakening to aesthetics. The turn of the century may well be called the "Bibelot Period," charmingly exemplified by the dainty books printed at the press of Thomas Bird Mosher (1852–1923), whose fastidious taste in literature complemented his judicious use of Caslon type, wide margins, and handmade papers.

The flood of tastefully designed books, many in reasonably priced limited editions, issuing from a great number of designers, printers, and small published houses, makes a bright chapter in the history of American graphic art. Then as now, personal publishing brought greater satisfaction than financial returns, and many imprints survived a very short time. Most successful in leaving their mark upon publishing were Herbert Stuart Stone and Hannibal Ingalls Kimball, who together and separately, from 1893 to 1905, published about three hundred books and three magazines. Stone and Kimball freely commissioned work from the best available talent and paid particular attention to their bindings.

The introduction of case-making machines in the nineties gave impetus to edition binding as a separate branch of graphic art. Such bindings, tastefully blocked in two or more colors and including white and gold, were a refreshing change from the overly ornate designs of mid-century. Most novels were bound in decorative covers and also illustrated by the best artists. One of the earliest cover designers was Margaret Neilson Armstrong (1867–1944), who dominated the field and had done at least 257 covers before 1913. Decorative binding languished with the introduction of book jackets.

The invention of the gasoline engine was to profoundly affect graphic art and advertising in future decades. Life in America changed radically with the arrival of the automobile. Public excitement over auto races, sensationally reported in the press, was almost overnight transformed into more personal excitement as thousands of citizens took to the road in their new gas buggies. The production of cars rose from 5,000 in 1900 to 600,000 in 1914. Production-line methods made cars easier to own, and the great potential of advertising was thoroughly exploited by automobile manufacturers; in 1915 the automobile industry took first rank among national advertisers, holding the lead over food advertising for another twenty-five years or more.

Outdoor advertising expanded into the countryside to catch the eye of motorists chugging along freshly paved roads. By 1912 a standard size of a little more than 8 by 19 feet for bulletin boards had been adopted; these could be filled with complete posters assembled from 24 lithographed sheets. The 24-sheet poster could be printed economically in great quantities and posted from coast to coast.

With the entry of the U.S. into the World War in August, 1914, the graphic arts shifted dramatically to propaganda. Art schools all over the country established poster classes and contributed poster designs by the thousands. A committee comprising nearly every notable illustrator and designer in the New York area turned out over seven hundred designs without fees of any kind. Posters for about fifty different war agencies, including recruitment, war bonds, and the Red Cross, were printed by the millions. It was the poster artist's finest hour, marked by some of the greatest and most famous posters of all time.

World War I posters, predominantly pictorial, reflected the current emphasis on illustration in all advertising, with perhaps too much copy playing a secondary role. A notable exception was the work of Fred G. Cooper, who blazed a new trail by eliminating all illustration and using exaggerated lettering as the principal element of design. The use of hand-drawn lettering in many styles reached a high point of perfection after the war.

The demonstrated power of World War I propaganda convinced institutions, public utilities companies, and trade associations that the same techniques could be profitably used in public relations for peacetime purposes. What we now call institutional or cooperative publicity has since contributed a fertile field to the practice of graphic design.

Two other methods of reproduction used during this period must be mentioned: photogravure and collotype. Photogravure is an intaglio halftone process based upon the principle of etching and copper or steel engraving, in which variations of tone are achieved by printing from a plate containing a photographically produced meshwork of tiny cells of varying depths. The deeper the cell, the more ink it contains for the paper to receive when the impression is made. Photogravure was widely used during the early part of this century for reproduction of fine art and art photographs. When the process was adapted to cylinder printing, or *rotogravure,* including color, it was extensively used in the printing of some magazines and Sunday supplements.

The only known photographic process for printing continuous tones without use of a halftone screen is collotype. During the course of its development since 1855, it was known by various names: Albertype, Phototype, Photogelatine, Heliochrome, and others. Essentially, it is a planographic process similar to lithography but with a printing surface coated with lightsensitive gelatine. The complete absence of anything except a verticulated grain makes it ideal for the reproduction of fine art except for the fact that extreme care and great skill are necessary for good results. In September, 1890, the Meriden Gravure Company imported its first collotype presses from Germany, giving them the lead in development of the process. Experimentation with an offset press in the late thirties demonstrated that even better work could be done by printing from offset plates using an extremely fine screen of 300 lines per inch. They also succeeded in the offset gravure reproduction of color subjects with remarkable fidelity and richness. The firm is now a principal producer of art reproductions for museums and fine books.

214

A special group of periodicals catered to the new
opulence of the early twentieth century; among
them *Country Life* and *Theatre Magazine,*
measuring ten by fourteen inches. Their back
covers were emblazoned with poster-size pro-
nouncements addressed to the wealthy. The
Pierce Arrow Company contracted for this

The Pierce Arrow

215

valuable space on an annual basis from 1907 to
1912 and engaged the country's most notable
illustrators. These included Edward Penfield
(214), Adolph Treidler (215), J. C. Leyendecker
(216), Louis Fancher, Robert Wildhack, and
Jack Sheridan.

216

A PORTFOLIO OF
BRADLEY'S TYPOGRAPHIC DESIGNS

Will Bradley's name shines brightly in the annals of American graphic art; few have contributed such a wide variety of new design patterns for others to follow. He was one of the first artists to introduce Art Nouveau to the American public. During the Art Poster craze of the 1890s, his posters ranked with the best produced in France. He was a fine printer with a flair for novel arrangements of type and innovative decoration, and he was the originator of the chapbook style of printing, which quickly evolved into a popular medium for advertising. Some of his most characteristic and charming creations were the ornaments and typecast cuts he designed for the famous chapbooks issued by the American Typefounders Company early in this century. Though a frail man, his productivity and versatility were phenomenal; he wrote and illustrated books, designed a huge quantity of outstanding advertising material, and from his own studio handled the art editorships of as many as five or six magazines at a time.

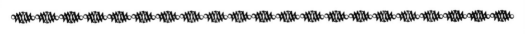

 # American
Type Founders Company
U. S. America

217

Handsome wedding of hand-lettering with delicately drawn decoration by Bradley. The rendering of the tailpieces (218, 220, 221) shows a distinctively personal interpretation by the artist, using naturalistic and conventional forms in his individualistic style.

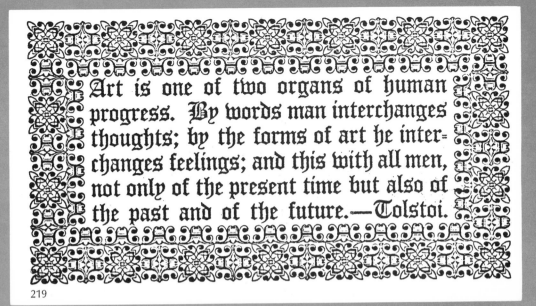

Art is one of two organs of human progress. By words man interchanges thoughts; by the forms of art he inter=changes feelings; and this with all men, not only of the present time but also of the past and of the future.—Tolstoi.

219

A LADY OF QUALITY

Being a most curious, hitherto unknown history, as related by Mr. Isaac Bickerstaff but not presented to the World of Fashion through the pages of *The Tatler*, and now for the first time written down *by*

Frances Hodgson Burnett

New York: From the Publishing House of CHARLES SCRIBNER'S SONS, 153-157 Fifth Avenue. *MDCCCXCVII.*

220

THE SEATS OF THE MIGHTY

BEING the Memoirs of *Captain* ROBERT MORAY, Sometime an *Officer* in the VIRGINIA Regiment, & afterwards of AMHERST's Regiment.

By GILBERT PARKER, Esq.

AUTHOR OF *Pierre and His People, When Valmond Came to Pontiac, The Trail of the Sword, The Trespasser, Etc.*

New York: D. APPLETON AND COMPANY. *Mdcccxcvii*

221

The Delectable
Art *of*
𝕻rinting:
CALLED ALSO
𝕿he 𝕻rinter 𝕸an's 𝕵oy:
TREATING
Of the *Origination* and Founding of
CHAP-BOOK BORDERS AND ORNAMENTS;
Of Pleasing Arrangements and the Appropriate
Use of Certain Styles;

Of the Variety and Surpassing Beauty which
the PRINTER may produce with
Simple Means; and of the

𝕾atisfaction and 𝕻rofit
of Doing the Same;

TO WHICH IS ADDED A
List of the Types & Characters
Needful, and How They may
be obtained; and, also,
the Cost thereof.

PUBLISHED BY THE
AMERICAN Type Founders Company
A. D. 1905

All these specimens are from a most successful brochure by Bradley for the American Type Founders Company, issued in 1905. The harmonious coordination of design, type, typographic ornaments, and chapbook figures inspired a Colonial revival in printers everywhere.

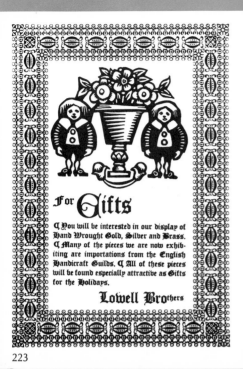

For **Gifts**

❡ You will be interested in our display of Hand Wrought Gold, Silver and Brass. ❡ Many of the pieces we are now exhibiting are importations from the English Handicraft Guilds. ❡ All of these pieces will be found especially attractive as Gifts for the Holidays.

Lowell Brothers

223

MOODS

A BOOK OF VERSE

224

FRANK WARE

A Drummer

Representing

WARD & DAY

Musical Instruments

NEW YORK

225

Style

Green 8 Hollison State St.

This was once in vogue but is now somewhat out of fashion. Styles that have been adopted as modes for the coming season will be displayed in our parlors during the first week of April.

226

227

J · O · H · N H · B · R · O · W · N
Printer
BROAD ST.   LYNBROOK

228

ROBERTS FRUIT COMPANY
JAMES W. ROBERTS   RALPH L. ROBERTS

BROMFIELD AND MONROE STREETS, WESTCHESTER

All's Well!

The Rider
Pharmacy is just
like home to those
College Students
who want the best
kind of drugs and
such other goods
as are only found
in up-to-date phar-
macies. The best
attention is given
to the filling of all
prescriptions with
pure drugs. C. L.
Rider, Proprietor
Evanstown, Ohio

229

DON'T FORGET THE
BAND
CONCERT

OR THE BIG STOCK OF
CLOTHING
AT BROWMAN'S

230

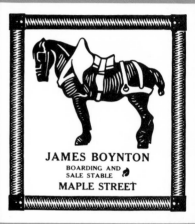

JAMES BOYNTON
BOARDING AND
SALE STABLE
MAPLE STREET

231

233

SURPRISED?
*Well, so is everybody when
they see the big bargains we
have to offer. Our stock was
never so large as at present,
and it embraces everything
of the very best kind from a
tin dipper to a cooking stove.*
CASH HARDWARE CO.

232

FRANK WARE
A Drummer

Representing
WARD & DAY
Musical Instruments
NEW YORK

Bradley's promotional pieces for the typefoundry,
all of which he designed and supervised, dis-
pelled the staid Victorian tastelessness then
prevalent. He introduced a fresh note that swept
out all vestiges of nineteenth-century practices
and made the printer's typecases obsolete.

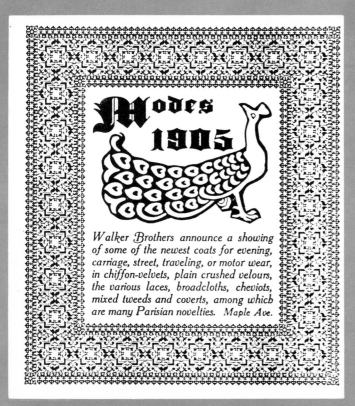

Walker Brothers announce a showing
of some of the newest coats for evening,
carriage, street, traveling, or motor wear,
in chiffon-velvets, plain crushed velours,
the various laces, broadcloths, cheviots,
mixed tweeds and coverts, among which
are many Parisian novelties. Maple Ave.

Sweets to the Sweet

We have the
Choicest Line of **Candies** In the City
J. H. Smith & Company

Don't be Downcast

That matter of a suitable gift need not worry
you. The Burnham Co. have just received
from the St. Louis Exposition, and have
placed on sale, the splendid collection of
Silverware, Goldware, Jewelry, and Leather
Goods, comprising their entire exhibit, and
for which they were awarded seven Grand
Prizes, and seven Gold Medals. Now, for
the first time, offered for sale. We have made
special arrangements for the delivery of any
selection from our stock at a future date, and
shipping details will be carefully attended to.

THE BURNHAM COMPANY
Woodlawn Avenue, Cleveland

Bell Phone
242. 2

BE JOLLY
But Don't be
JOLLIED

You are jolly when you buy
and use the kind of *printing
that brings results*, you are
jollied when you are led to
believe that poor printing is
cheap printing, and that such
printing pays. The printing
of the Aldine Press is *good
printing*, and because it is
good printing it is CHEAP.

Aldine Press
Joy Avenue

The *KNICKERBOCKER* HISTORY OF *NEW YORK*

Book iv.
Chapter One

SHOWING THE NATURE OF HISTORY IN GENERAL;
CONTAINING FURTHERMORE THE UNIVERSAL
ACQUIREMENTS OF WILLIAM THE TESTY, AND
HOW A MAN MAY KNOW SO MUCH AS TO
RENDER HIMSELF GOOD FOR NOTHING

WHEN the lofty Thucydides is about to enter upon his description of the plague that desolated Athens, one of his modern commentators assures the reader that the history is now going to be exceeding solemn, serious and pathetic, and hints, with that air of chuckling gratulation with which a good dame draws forth a choice morsel from a cupboard to regale a favorite, that this plague will give his history a most agreeable variety.

In like manner did my heart leap within me when I came to the dolorous dilemma of Fort Good Hope, which I at once perceived to be the forerunner of a series of great events and entertaining disasters. Such are the true subjects for the historic pen. For what is history, in fact, but a kind of a Newgate Calendar, a register of crimes and miseries that man has inflicted on his fellow man? It is a huge libel on human nature, to which we industriously add page after page, volume after volume, as if we were building up a monument to the honor rather than the infamy of our species. If we turn over the pages of these chronicles that man has written of himself, what are the characters dignified by the appellation of great, and held up to the admiration of posterity? Tyrants, robbers, conquerors, renowned only for the magnitude of their misdeeds and the stupendous wrongs and miseries they have inflicted on mankind.

238

In this book page Will Bradley has recreated an appropriate Colonial atmosphere with liberal use of italic capitals and swash characters, printers' flowers and foundry cuts, and the interjection of chapter numbers in gothics. Black and white stipple illustrations for this edition, first issued in 1903, were executed by Maxfield Parrish.

A PORTFOLIO OF
EARLY MAGAZINE COVERS

The popularity of the poster technique is reflected in many of the covers designed for turn-of-the-century magazines. Often dominated by a single figure, the cover became a poster in miniature. Decoration was also used for dressing up covers displaying contents in carefully arranged type or hand lettering. Cover designers were among the first to utilize newly improved printing processes.

239

240

Edward Penfield's cover for *Collier's* (240) is the epitome of poster simplicity, the graceful, rhythmic stride of the hound keeping pace with his mistress. The *Scribner's* cover by Robert J. Wildhack (241) expresses, appropriately, the blowy March day, dated 1906.

Guernsey Moore

The annual automobile number was a regular feature of many national magazines of the day; designed by Guernsey Moore in 1909. The *Metropolitan* cover (243), one of over a hundred covers designed by Penfield, shows the smartly tailored type he became known for.

METROPOLITAN MAGAZINE

June 1909   Price 15 cents

The cover designs by Maxfield Parrish exhibit the talent of one of America's great illustrators. The quaint book-lover (244), drawn in 1910, shows Parrish using one of his favorite devices—patterning to avoid shades and shadows. The botanist cover appeared in 1908.

Colli∎r's

THE ∎ATION∎∎ ∎EEKLY

M . P

246

James Montgomery Flagg cancelled most of his profitable magazine commissions to devote himself wholeheartedly to the war effort. His pointing Uncle Sam (246) is generally considered the most famous poster of the war. Four million copies were distributed, and it was also used nearly as extensively, in various forms, during World War II.

A PORTFOLIO OF
WORLD WAR I POSTERS

During the First World War the patriotic fervor of Americans found magnificent expression in thousands of posters created by professional designers and illustrators who contributed their talents without charge. Some of the greatest posters of all time were commissioned by the Division of Pictorial Publicity and printed by the millions.

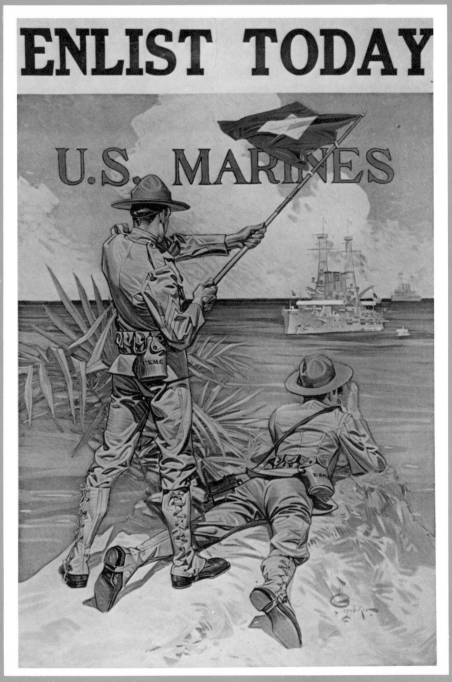

USA BONDS

Third
Liberty Loan
Campaign
BOY SCOUTS
OF AMERICA

WEAPONS FOR LIBERTY

248

One of the most unforgettable posters of the War (248), this Liberty Loan appeal painted by J. C. Leyendecker honors the Boy Scouts of America for their efforts in selling bonds. The nobility of the concept, the semiallegorical grouping, the statuesque beauty of Miss Liberty and the handsome, well-poised scout, all combine to deliver an inspiring message. In the "Order Coal Now" poster (249) Leyendecker's crisp, painterly technique, familiar to millions from his *Saturday Evening Post* covers, succeeds in rendering an ordinary subject dramatically.

249

250

251

252

253

A variety of posters vastly different in appeal, subject matter, and technique were created by many artists: J. Allen St. John (250); Charles Livingston Bull (251); Unknown artist (252); Ellsworth Young (253); Scott Williams (254); Henry P. Raleigh (255); Adolph Treidler (256).

254

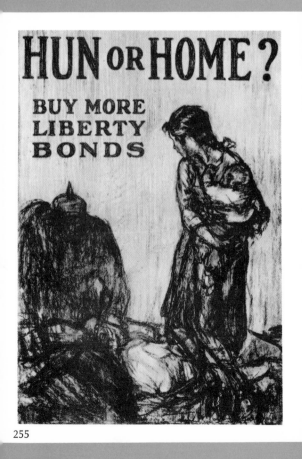

255

256

BOOKS WANTED FOR OUR MEN IN CAMP AND "OVER THERE" TAKE YOUR GIFTS TO THE PUBLIC LIBRARY

257

Charles B. Falls created this poster (257) for the American Library Association on 24 hour notice. It has been cited as one of the finest ever done in this country, fulfilling the artist's concept for the poster: "A poster should be to the eye what a shouted command is to the ear."

Joseph Pennell, noted book and magazine illustrator, lithographer, and architectural draftsman, portrays in his Fourth Liberty Loan poster (258) an enemy force destroying New York City and the Statue of Liberty. A convincing realism strongly emphasizes the message.

JOSEPH PENNELL DEL.

THAT LIBERTY SHALL NOT PERISH FROM THE EARTH BUY LIBERTY BONDS
FOURTH LIBERTY LOAN

258

259

Within the first quarter of the twentieth century
the motor car, having passed through its awk-
ward, formative years—when the big question
to be settled was "Will it be powered by electric,
steam, or gas?"—had reached full maturity. The
automobile was finally an accepted part of life,
common in the most remote regions of our land.
For a nation on wheels the only question

remaining was "Which car shall I buy?" The
auto makers and their enterprising advertising
agents addressed themselves fully to this billion-
dollar opportunity, pouring forth countless pages
in the daily press and national periodicals. Along
with the proliferation of magazine pages there
was an equally profitable production of fine
booklets and sales catalogs.

1920·1950

GOLDEN DAYS OF ADVERTISING

To MOST of us "the roaring Twenties" is synonymous with the era of Prohibition, when liquor went underground; of bootleggers, speakeasies, and bathtub gin. It was the old wild west among the skyscrapers, floating on a lagoon of illicit booze, rocking with the sound of jazz.

Lacerations in the social fabric were minutely described in the novels of F. Scott Fitzgerald; the new look documented in the unforgettable drawings of John Held, Jr. (1889–1958). Held set the style; his flappers and college boys became the prototypes of modern youth, symbols of revolt against old standards. Girls bobbed their hair and wore little more than ropes of beads and scandalously short dresses. The boyish figure was in; bosoms were out of style. When the first Beauty Pageant was held at Atlantic City, September 7, 1921, the Miss America crown went to Margaret Gorman, whose bust was considerably smaller than her hips—a trend not to be reversed until the thirties.

Beginning in the twenties, the graphic arts underwent many transformations in character, keeping in step with a prosperous economy providing greatly expanded as well as new opportunities for graphic expression: motion picture advertising, direct mail campaigns, industrial and corporate design, and a wide range of product promotions from distinctive packaging and point-of-purchase display to book jackets and record covers.

The crosscurrents of new dimensions in fine art, architecture, and decoration were so numerous and varied as to discourage any definitive attempt to sort out their influence on the graphic arts.

Art Deco was a reaction against Art Nouveau and had its roots in the Arts and Crafts Movement. Functionalism rejected opulent curves and complicated construction in favor of geometric shapes more suitable to mass production. In furniture design and in architecture, the emphasis was on flat and highly polished surfaces, with sheets of glass and exotic materials as integral parts of the construction. Art Deco, as the term implies, was thought

149

of principally as the decoration of such surfaces. This preoccupation with surface decoration opened the way to a great variety of exotic motifs—Oriental, Egyptian, Aztec, among others—which were subsequently adapted to graphic design. Not so happily adapted from Art Deco was a rash of trendy typefaces like Broadway (ATF, 1929), combining fat, geometrical shapes with excessively thin lines, now being revived for their nostalgic appeal despite their illegibility.

Graphic art also borrowed ideas and design principles derived from Cubism, Futurism, and abstract art, involving repetition of form, color, and line; continuity of line; curves against straight edges; warm color against cold; dark against light; and conversion of perspective into two-dimensional planes which appear to penetrate each other. These principles sparked a significant departure from traditional formats in layout and pictorial representation.

Dada was founded in 1916 at Zurich by a group of disillusioned artists and writers who set out to ridicule established criterions. Meant to shock the public out of its complacency, Dadaist anti-art emphasized the illogical and absurd, in which chance played an important role in the haphazard mixture of disparate elements, including collages assembled from pictures clipped from magazines and catalogues. Dadaist printing completely disregarded accepted rules of horizontal typography.

To the above catalogue of influences upon the graphic arts must be added Surrealism, Constructivism, and the broad spectrum of experiments carried on at the Bauhaus, founded at Weimar by Walter Gropius in 1919.

Out of this ferment came a general departure from the vertically symmetrical division of space in advertising and typographic layout, an outworn tradition ill-suited to the new technology. What was needed was a typographic format sympathetic to machine composition, and to complement it, new type forms. German designers were the leaders in the "new typography," which was essentially functional and, with asymmetrical arrangement of copy blocks and display lines, suggestive of the rectangular or gridlike paintings of Piet Mondrian.

The appearance in 1927 of Paul Renner's *Futura,* the first successful "modern" typeface, caused a sensation in typographic circles. Based on the geometric principles of compass and straight-edge, its mechanical perfection softened by the most subtle adjustments, it was the ideal type for contemporary expression. Enormously successful, it overshadowed Rudolf Koch's *Kabel* of the same period. Similar sans-serifs, under such names as *Metro, Vogue, Tempo,* and *Spartan* followed in quick succession; the last-named is the most widely used in this country.

Indicative of the prosperity and pursuit of pleasure during the twenties were the extravagantly elaborate musical reviews like the Ziegfeld Follies, the dance craze, sports cars, and the burgeoning of glossy magazines catering to the affluent and sophisticated. *Vogue* and *Harper's Bazaar* were arbiters of fashion. After 1929 *Vanity Fair,* under the art direction of M. F. Agha, blazed new trails in magazine layout; it was widely publicized as an impressive *tour-de-force* of all-embracing graphic organization. Despite the stock market crash of November, 1929, *Fortune,* completely designed by T. M. Cleland and selling for a dollar a copy, was a financial success.

New and old magazines revealed a new synthesis of editorial content and graphics; many gifted designers entered the field. Paper manufacturers produced elaborate promotion material under the guidance of distinguished designers. Most notable was *Westvaco Inspirations,* assiduously collected and studied by graphic artists.

Since the early twenties, *The Annual of Advertising Art,* still being published by the Art Directors Club of New York, has recorded new trends. Earlier volumes show a preponderance of work by illustrators in all mediums, including the unique pen drawings of Franklin Booth and a dazzling array of highly decorative cartouches and borders by such masters of line-works as T. M. Cleland, Walter Dorwin Teague, Clarence P. Hornung, Carlton Ellinger, O. W. Jaquish, and the Rosa brothers. These Annuals also show signs of the impending photographic revolution, which was to increasingly preempt the work of illustrators in advertising. It was principally in story illustration that illustrators held their ground, though the work of such outstanding artists as Maxfield Parrish (1870–1966), Coles Phillips (1880–1927), and J. C. Leyendecker (1874–1951) came to be associated in the public mind with certain extensively advertised products.

The flowering of the graphic arts has been nourished through exhibitions, educational programs, and printed material sponsored by professional organizations from coast to coast. The American Institute of Graphic Arts (AIGA) is the most important of such organizations as well as the only one which is truly national in scope. Founded in 1914 in New York, its membership is composed of those who are professionally engaged in work with the graphic arts and includes typographers, book designers, illustrators, publishers, printers, bookbinders, platemakers, and suppliers of materials that go into the making of books.

The AIGA holds a continuing series of exhibits in both the United States and abroad. The most important of these is the "Fifty Books of the Year" show; inclusion in it is a much coveted honor. The highest honor of all has been the Institute Medal of Award, presented from time to time for distinguished contributions to the progress of the Graphic Arts. Members receive show catalogues, announcements, booklets, and special keepsakes which are themselves notable examples of graphic art. Throughout the year are educational courses, lectures and round-table discussions, workshop sessions, and a variety of meetings devoted to special subjects.

Chicago's preeminence as a center of graphic arts and printing is underscored by the existence, since 1927, of the Society of Typographic Arts (STA). Chicago can boast of an impressive roster of distinguished graphic artists, consistently supported by interested local institutions and corporations as clients and sponsors of educational programs. The result has been a unique independence from New York's influence and a definite "Chicago Style" of graphic design. The STA annual exhibitions, displaying superb work in all departments of graphic art done in the Chicago area, attract world-wide attention.

Consumer magazines reaped a rich harvest in advertising revenue, underwriting the careers of an unprecedented number of distinguished artists. The leader in this respect was *The Saturday Evening Post;* Norman Rockwell's famous *Post* covers began to appear as early as May 20, 1916. The *Post* led in bulk as well, notably in a December, 1929, issue containing 272 pages and weighing almost two pounds. Sixty 45-ton presses rolled round the clock for three weeks to produce it, consuming six million pounds of paper and 120,000 pounds of ink.

In book design the Kelmscott vogue for overloaded decoration waned soon after 1900, but there began to appear a new generation of graphic artists and printers imbued with the principles of unified design and sound craftsmanship enunciated by William Morris; a large proportion were to achieve international reputations. Nearly all broadened their talents through close study and practical experience in all phases of book production.

Will Bradley, already noted, was largely responsible for the popularity of the chapbook style of printing. His talents were like a bottomless well from which issued a prodigious flow of fresh ideas in typographic layout and ornament, typefaces, books, magazine covers and formats.

Frederic W. Goudy (1865–1947), despite setbacks and two disastrous fires, gained great distinction as a printer and writer on typographic subjects, and particularly as a prolific type designer, having created well over a hundred typefaces. T. M. Cleland (1880–1964) was in great demand for his meticulously rendered and highly sophisticated decorations for books and advertising. His typographic work was a superb blend of exquisite taste and the finest traditions of printing. Bruce Rogers (1870–1957) is asserted to have done more to make everyday books readable and beautiful than any other single individual in modern times. He was master of allusive typography and decoration, and the more than four hundred books produced under his care were perfect expressions of their content. W. A. Dwiggins

(1880–1956) is hard to define. He was a calligrapher, typographer and type designer, book designer and illustrator, author and puppeteer. He excelled in each, combining whimsy with sound craftsmanship, decorating his books in a highly individual style.

Interest in first editions and fine books as subjects for collecting reached a high pitch during the twenties. Numerous publishers capitalized on the new trend by issuing limited and signed editions at inflated prices hardly justified by expensive paper, wider margins, and "special" bindings. More discriminating collectors rejected these artificial rarities in favor of books distinguished for the excellence of their typography and printing. The swelling market for such books created a salubrious climate in which gifted designers and quality printers flourished.

For some time, various private groups had been issuing specially commissioned fine books for members only. In 1929, George Macy launched The Limited Editions Club, offering to 1,500 yearly subscribers one new edition of a literary classic per month. Each volume was to cost $15.00 and be produced under the direction of the best designers, illustrators, and printers. His venture was an artistic success. Later he published attractive but popularly priced books under the Heritage Press imprint, and *The Dolphin,* a short-lived but distinguished series on typography and book design.

Another manifestation of renewed interest in fine printing was the appearance in 1930 of *The Colophon: A Book Collector's Quarterly.* Bound in decorated boards, each volume was made up of sections produced by various distinguished printers and designers. In New York, the Typophiles, growing out of a luncheon club of printing enthusiasts, began a cooperative program for issuing a notable series of chapbooks and monographs in 1935.

Inevitably all forms of graphic art benefited from these enterprises, finding in book production new and exciting outlets for original work in mediums that had long been neglected during the rise of photoengraving. The willingness of a large segment of the public to pay more money for attractive books in limited editions encouraged otherwise too expensive experiments in the use of rubber plates for printing with watercolor inks, and the coloring of illustrations by means of stencils.

Trade book publishers—notably Alfred A. Knopf—were stimulated to employ top designers to improve the layouts and bindings of their books. The new firm of Random House created quite a stir in 1928 by issuing as its first imprint a limited edition of *Candide,* illustrated and signed by Rockwell Kent. Hand-set in a new roman type designed by Lucian Bernhard and produced by Pynson Printers, it remains a high-spot in printing and publishing history.

Salon
DE LA MODE

260

Setting the pace in design for printers and advertisers were a number of better paper manufacturers. They pointed the way in their use of brochures, folders, printed forms, and house organs designed to initiate trends in the graphic arts. Of these two examples the Eagle–A papers (260) were printed in soft shades of lavender, orange, and black. The Collins Laidtone folder cover (261) suggests the delicately engraved nielloesques of seventeenth-century goldsmiths.

154

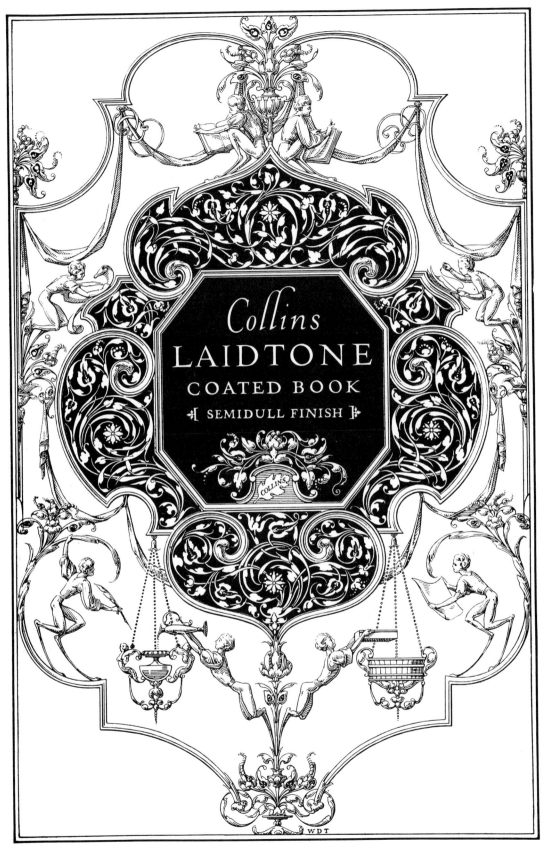

Collins
LAIDTONE
COATED BOOK
⊰[SEMIDULL FINISH]⊱

COLLINS

WDT

261

262

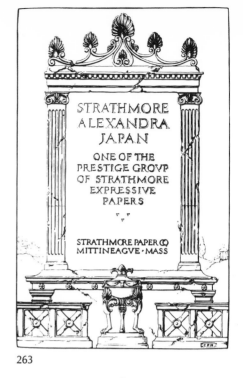

263

264

265

The advertising designer of the twenties had a broad choice of historic styles to choose from when planning a printed piece. How he exercised this eclecticism was a test of his versatility and craftsmanship in a demanding profession. The salon announcement for Rolls-Royce (262) was executed in the austere manner of a Pompeiian fresco decoration. The cover of the Strathmore piece (263) was done as an antique Roman entablature with lettering to simulate an incised inscription. The Antique Silver announcement for B. Altman (264) exhibits a decorative composition done with grace and delicacy. For the artist's removal notice (265) he invokes the Italianate manner of Mantegna. All were designed about 1925 by Clarence P. Hornung. The exhibition announcement of Carlton D. Ellinger (266), noted graphic artist, in elaborate strapwork interlaced with scrolls and leaf forms, is a tour de force.

A PORTFOLIO OF
DECORATIVE ADVERTISING

One of the unique results of the Golden Age of advertising was the creation of decorative designs and borders for the printed page. A number of distinguished artists rendered these in carefully delineated penlines, adroitly adapting historic styles of ornamentation to embellish the message. True works of art, the examples that follow are in the finest tradition of master ornamentalists.

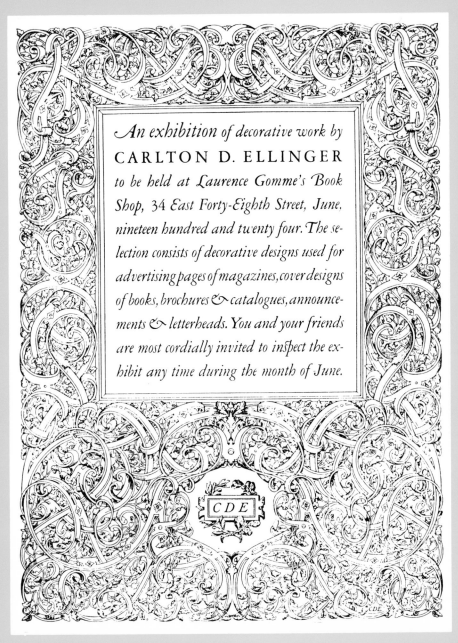

266

267

The Rolls-Royce advertisement (267), styled in the finest tradition of the French engravers, was created in 1924 by Thomas M. Cleland. Disdaining even the hint of an automobile—thus achieving status and distinction—the artist's lofty setting is a classical palace reminiscent of a Bibiena or Piranesi. Cleland's theatricality is again obvious in the stage set for Locomobile (268). Here the designer invokes his best Pompeiian manner to wed copy and classic decoration.

LOCOMOBILE

PRE NVMERO EXCELLENTIA

*E*quipage and Furniture were Fine Arts in Ancient Culture and throughout all periods of high civilization. Great Artists devoted to them the same enthusiasm as to sculpture, painting and architecture.

The Locomobile is similarly conceived. Artists have given it style and design, and artificers have produced it painstakingly, Car by Car.

$4700. to $9700.

THE LOCOMOBILE COMPANY OF AMERICA
MAKERS OF FINE MOTOR CARS

268

159

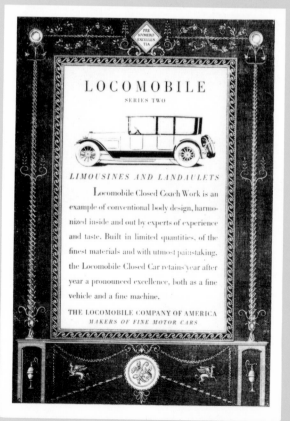

269

Noted for grace, luxury, and refinement, at a price tag approaching ten thousand dollars, Locomobile's advertising addressed its appeal to a limited few, conveyed in a series of decorative announcements of impeccable taste and superior craftsmanship (269–271). The copy stresses "excellence before numbers" in this custom-made automobile, relying upon the quiet dignity of the presentation.

271

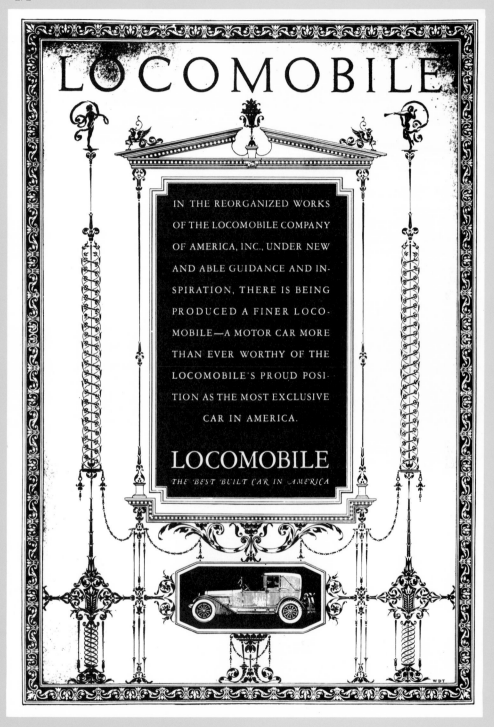

LOCOMOBILE

IN THE REORGANIZED WORKS
OF THE LOCOMOBILE COMPANY
OF AMERICA, INC., UNDER NEW
AND ABLE GUIDANCE AND IN-
SPIRATION, THERE IS BEING
PRODUCED A FINER LOCO-
MOBILE—A MOTOR CAR MORE
THAN EVER WORTHY OF THE
LOCOMOBILE'S PROUD POSI-
TION AS THE MOST EXCLUSIVE
CAR IN AMERICA.

LOCOMOBILE
THE BEST BUILT CAR IN AMERICA

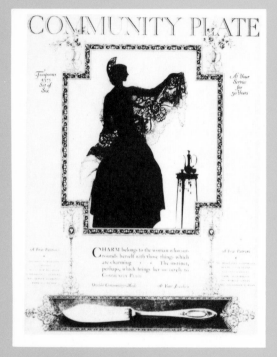

273

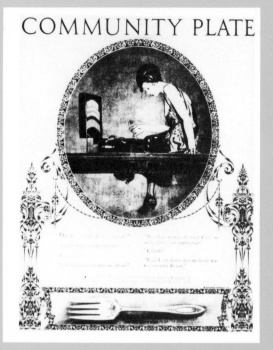

274

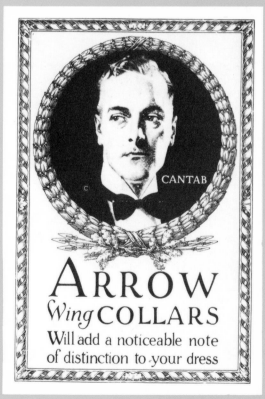

275

KEBO

ARROW COLLARS

are designed for men who are particular in all matters
pertaining to dress & who acknowledge the fitness of
no substitute for Arrow the collar of the gentleman

Cluett, Peabody & Co. Inc. Makers Troy N.Y.

276

277

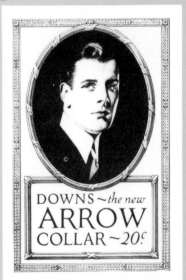

DOWNS ~ *the new*
ARROW
COLLAR ~ *20¢*

During the 1920s the advertisements for Community Plate appearing in national publications
promoted beauty of design in tableware appointments. The decorative frames sometimes enclosed
a painting by Coles Phillips, an interior of a
lovely home, or a photo of some well-known
beauty. The pages from the pen of Walter D.
Teague (273, 274) achieved outstanding success
by combining various elements to promote the
idea of quality, taste, and refinement. Another
noted group of advertisements featured designs
by Teague as a background frame for J. C.
Leyendecker's celebrated portraits of "the Arrow
Collar man" (275–277), which appeared
nationally in the mid-twenties.

278

Another noteworthy group of decorative advertisements by Teague (278, 279) were commissioned by the firm making Adler-Rochester clothes, leaders in their field. Decorative design is used to a degree seldom seen at the time. In its psychology of association, instead of style appeal, it creates an atmosphere of character by inference. The art of the garment maker is likened to the vase makers of Sevres, the lace makers of Brussels, or Stradivari of Cremona. That most elusive ingredient, quality, is inherent throughout. The versatile genius of Walter D. Teague created all the advertising pages for Phoenix Hosiery (280–283), its format quite differently styled from other campaigns running concurrently. The advertising message, set in large, clear, readable Goudy Oldstyle type, was embellished with a variety of well-planned design forms utilizing liberal white space and gray areas of intricate floral arabesques and rinceaux. Great ingenuity and linear mastery is evident in the rich, intriguing, naturalistic forms.

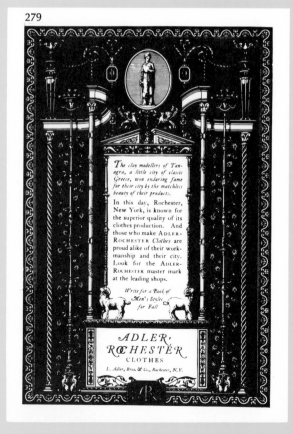

279

280

One half of your lifetime, and more, is spent in hosiery. Your constant and intimate traveling companion! It is an important part of your personal protection and embellishment. The world buys more Phoenix hosiery than any other kind, because it has *downright elegance* and a tenacious wear-ability that makes it a substantial economy. For men, women and children, it is the *standard* hosiery throughout the world.

PHOENIX
HOSIERY
MILWAUKEE

281

Neither romance nor history tells us who made the first pair of stockings. But certain it is that human progress is indicated by the remarkable refinements that have been made in hosiery. Never before this very day have men, women and children been able to own such beautiful and substantial foot-coverings at so low a cost. Phoenix leadership in this advancement has made it the standard hosiery of the world. But neither romance nor history can record the down-right satisfaction that has come from the long miles of strenuous and refined travel which this splendid product economically supplies.

PHOENIX
HOSIERY
MILWAUKEE

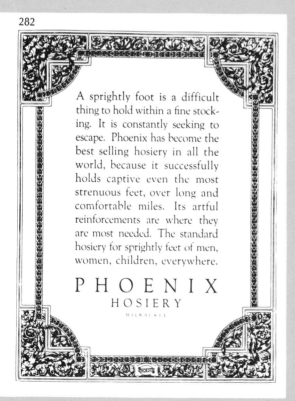

282

A sprightly foot is a difficult thing to hold within a fine stocking. It is constantly seeking to escape. Phoenix has become the best selling hosiery in all the world, because it successfully holds captive even the most strenuous feet, over long and comfortable miles. Its artful reinforcements are where they are most needed. The standard hosiery for sprightly feet of men, women, children, everywhere.

PHOENIX
HOSIERY
MILWAUKEE

283

Will your Christmas stocking, in this happy year, hold more than ever before? At your service, here and now, is a stocking that *will hold more*. Sturdiness! The outstanding fact about *Phoenix* hosiery is that it carries those who walk within it over record miles, in elegance, and at low cost. This world's most wanted hosiery is made in all the modish shades of silk, and silk-and-wool, for men, women and children. "The one complete line"—it is sold everywhere. Your Christmas stocking.

PHOENIX
HOSIERY
MILWAUKEE

Howard Pyle's Book of The American Spirit

The Romance of American History
Pictured by Howard Pyle
Compiled by Merle Johnson: with
Narrative Descriptive Text from
Original Sources *Edited by*
Francis J. Dowd

Harper & Brothers *Publishers*
New York & London MCMXXIII

THE DOOR IN THE WALL
And Other Stories

BY

H·G·WELLS

ILLUSTRATED
WITH PHOTOGRAVURES FROM
PHOTOGRAPHS BY

ALVIN LANGDON COBURN

NEW YORK & LONDON
MITCHELL KENNERLEY
MCMXI

CATALOGUE
of Old, Rare & Curious

BOOKS

*printed previous
to the year* 1800
now to be had of

W. A. GOUGH
41 *East* 60*th Street*
NEW YORK CITY

286

The renaissance of interest that stimulated a general improvement in book printing is best demonstrated when examining the title page, the gateway in the architecture of the book. Here the designer puts his best foot forward and sets the pattern for other pages. The hand-lettered title of Howard Pyle's *Book of the American Spirit* (284) breaks away from tradition. An early book title page by Fred Goudy (285) shows a first use of the Kennerley type he especially designed and named for the publisher. The Gough catalog cover (286) displays a harmony of Caslon Antique with foundry ornaments designed by W. D. Teague. The title and opening page (287, 288) are the work of one of America's most distinguished book designers, Bruce Rogers. Will Dwiggins, noted for his highly personal decorative style as a book designer and calligrapher, designed and lettered the double title page (289).

THE
JOURNAL
OF
Madam KNIGHT

With an INTRODUCTORY NOTE by
GEORGE PARKER WINSHIP

BOSTON:
Printed by BRUCE ROGERS for the Publishers
SMALL, MAYNARD & COMPANY
1920

THE
JOURNAL
OF
Madam *KNIGHT.*

❖❖❖❖❖❖❖❖❖❖❖❖❖❖❖

Monday, Octb'r. y second,
1704.*

ABOUT three o'clock afternoon, I
begun my Journey from Boston
to New-Haven; being about two Hundred Mile. My Kinsman, Capt. Robert
Luist, waited on me as farr as Dedham,
where I was to meet y* Western post.
                                        I

T H E

'Time Machine

H. G. WELLS

AN INVENTION

*With a preface by the Author
written for this edition; and
designs by* W. A. Dwiggins

RANDOM HOUSE *New York*

THE
PAROCHIAL
LIBRARY
of the
Eighteenth Century
in
CHRIST CHURCH
BOSTON

By
A *Proprietor* of CHRIST CHURCH

BOSTON
Privately printed at the *Merrymount Press* in the
Year of our LORD MDCCCCXVII

THE
PREFACE
TO
Johnson's
DICTIONARY
OF THE
English Language
1755

CLEVELAND
THE ROWFANT CLUB
1934

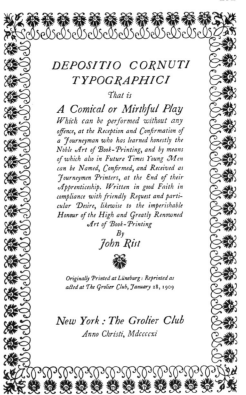

DEPOSITIO CORNUTI
TYPOGRAPHICI
That is

A Comical or Mirthful Play
Which can be performed without any
offence, at the Reception and Confirmation of
a Journeyman who has learned honestly the
Noble Art of Book-Printing, and by means
of which also in Future Times Young Men
can be Named, Confirmed, and Received as
Journeymen Printers, at the End of their
Apprenticeship. Written in good Faith in
compliance with friendly Request and parti-
cular Desire, likewise to the imperishable
Honour of the High and Greatly Renowned
Art of Book-Printing
By
John Rist

Originally Printed at Lüneburg: Reprinted as
acted at The Grolier Club, January 28, 1909

New York : The Grolier Club
Anno Christi, Mdccccxi

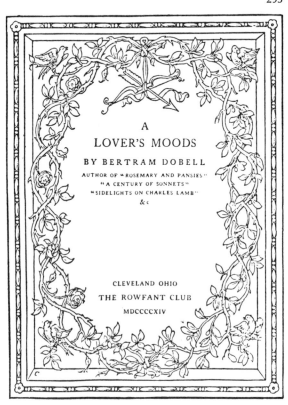

A
LOVER'S MOODS
BY BERTRAM DOBELL
AUTHOR OF "ROSEMARY AND PANSIES"
"A CENTURY OF SONNETS"
"SIDELIGHTS ON CHARLES LAMB"
&c

CLEVELAND OHIO
THE ROWFANT CLUB
MDCCCCXIV

The influence of one of America's great book printers should never be underestimated. Daniel Berkeley Updike and his Merrymount Press at Boston (290–293), in association with designers Bruce Rogers, Thomas Cleland, Theodore Hapgood, and Will Dwiggins, broadened his horizons to include decoration within a classical frame of reference. The title page for the Grolier Club publication (292) depends for decorative effect upon the border of fleurons and the use of italics throughout. Elsewhere (290–291) Updike arranges Caslon formally, greatly aided by an engraved panel of eighteenth-century ornament, and an oval cameo in wood-engraved fashion. For a title (293), he commissioned T. M. Cleland to design an appropriate setting of intertwined vines of rose and laurel. In the thirties a young group of book designers broke from the rigid classical traditions, using freer arrangements with new typefaces from abroad: Jane McCarthy (294); New Directions (295); George Van Vechten (296).

MODERN MEXICAN ART

LAURENCE E. SCHMECKEBIER

THE UNIVERSITY OF MINNESOTA PRESS, MINNEAPOLIS

Jean Garrigue

THE EGO AND THE CENTAUR

A New Directions Book

SCHNITZELBANK

METAMORPHOSED FROM THE ORIGINAL GERMAN WITH SKETCHES BY FRITZ KREDEL AND PRINTED BY THE PRESS OF THE WOOLLY WHALE IN NEW YORK CHRISTMAS MCMXXXVIII

298

299

J. C. Leyendecker made his first *Saturday
Evening Post* cover for the issue of May 20, 1899.
During the next forty years he became the most
important and popular cover artist for the
magazine, producing more than a dozen of them
each year at $1,500 each. His crisp, somewhat
stylized technique and sure decorative sense were
perfect for creating evocative designs to stimulate
newsstand sales. Altogether he painted 322
covers for the *Post,* including those for the
holiday numbers, for which he was regularly
commissioned. Millions looked forward to the
lively babies that symbolized the New Year for
almost four decades, each expressive of the most
engrossing topic of the day. Equally favored were
the paintings he made for the Easter, Independence Day, Thanksgiving, and Christmas
covers. Before Norman Rockwell, Leyendecker
was easily the most successful of all *Post* cover
artists.

300

301

302

In over sixty years of continuing popularity, Norman Rockwell and his work are unquestionably more familiar to the American public than any other artist in history. A prolific output of well over four hundred *Saturday Evening Post* covers alone has brought his talents into the homes of millions, many of whom have enjoyed no other contact with an artist of note. Certainly Rockwell is a phenomenon perennially in the forefront and is still, at over eighty, actively engaged in his pleasurable pursuits. But the primary interest in his genius, a wholesome grassroots sensibility, lies not in his masterful technique so much as in the subjects of his canvases. He is a storyteller without a peer, recording with "passionate accuracy and gentle humor" as Tom Buechner has said, those nostalgic situations known to each and every one of us—delicious bits of Americana that promise to live on in the hearts of all. From *Post* covers dated as follows: (301), 1923; (302), 1928; (303), 1929; (304), 1944.

303

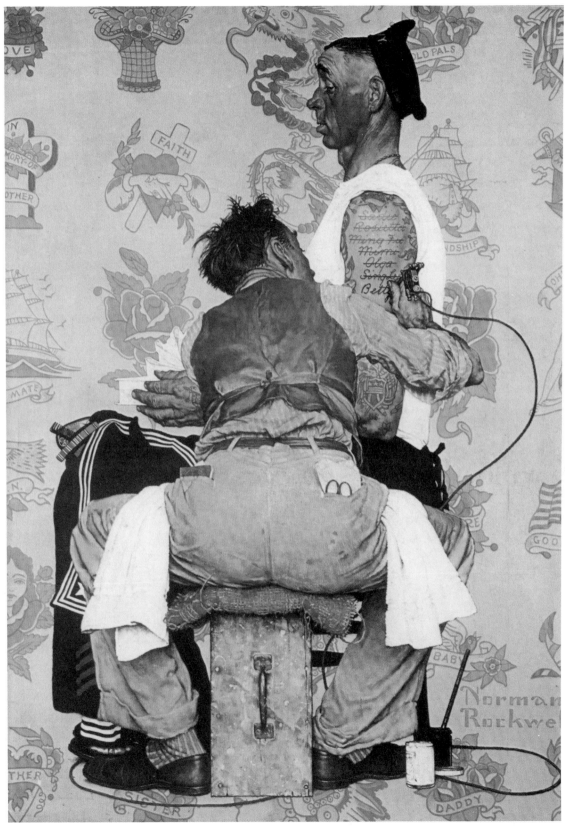

304

305

The times in which we are now living seem certain to be remembered as an epoch in which man took his first steps in space. Not since Columbus's time have men dared to enter more dangerous and mysterious regions. Whatever the eventual progress, man's venture into the outer regions is changing history in all its aspects. "When Apollo II left earth in July, 1969, to achieve man's first landing on the moon, the world watched through the medium of television. Among those present at Cape Kennedy were a group of artists who interpreted the historic event in their own way. Artists were at Houston in the control room during the landing on the moon and on the carrier in the Pacific for the splashdown. Thus we have a record for the future of some of the greatest moments of the present through a medium that is as old as our recorded past—the intimate human medium of the artist's eye and hand," wrote J. Carter Brown in his foreword to *Eyewitness to Space*. From a lithograph by John Meigs entitled *To the Moon*, from the collection of the National Aeronautics and Space Administration, 1963 to 1970.

1950-1975

THE CONTEMPORARY SCENE

LONG BEFORE 1950, the bustle of creativity in the graphic arts had lost momentum in some areas. The effect of the great Depression of the thirties was to severely curtail production of fine books and expensive typography. The younger generation of graphic artists had little incentive to emulate the great typographic designers and printers who, in spite of their international reputations, were obliged to close up shop or turn to more profitable and less demanding commercial work.

The character and direction of the graphic arts have always been affected by advances in printing and reproductive processes. During the past several decades, the most potent agents of change have been offset lithography and the camera. Ira Rubel, a Nutley, New Jersey, lithographer, noticed that when a feeder missed a sheet on his rotary press and the impression was made on the cylinder, the back of the sheet next to go through the press took the impression from the cylinder with remarkable sharpness. From this hint, Rubel devised the first offset press in 1905.

Perfecting the process took time and experimentation, branching off in two directions: various machines for cheap duplication in short runs, and larger, more complex offset presses for commercial printing. Essentially, offset printing is done from a flexible metal lithographic plate bearing a positive image, which is wrapped round a cylinder; it is inked, printed onto a rubber blanket, or roller, and the paper is printed from the roller.

The chief advantage of offset lithography is that the rubber roller prints uniformly on all kinds of paper, soft and subtle tones are possible, and a single light-weight litho plate substitutes for the more expensive and cumbersome lockups of heavy forms used for letterpress. Disadvantages are largely aesthetic; because the offset image lies on the surface of the paper, it lacks the sparkle and tactile appeal produced by the deep impression of fine relief printing. This is clearly demonstrated by comparing an original print of a wood engraving with its offset reproduction. Flat, grayish tones are characteristic of poor offset; under proper conditions the results in contrast and color reproduction are impressive, and the process continues to supplant letterpress for commercial work, books, magazines, and even some newspapers.

Offset printing having eliminated the need for anything more than a photographic image to place before the camera, preparation for it is largely a paste-up operation in which type proofs and all line work are assembled in proper position on a single mount. Halftones are screened separately; then all films are stripped together in their respective positions—for a single large sheet or for multiple pages—and the litho plate is made from it.

Reproduction proofs from conventional hand-set or machine composition are not necessary. Even ordinary typing with a clean black ribbon will do, though more satisfactory "proofs" are made on special typewriters. Savings in typesetting costs have thus been a boon to amateur journalists and publishers of lists and booklets who are more interested in economy than appearance.

A large proportion of typography for offset is now done photographically by a variety of machines activated by computers. They can be programmed to follow complicated instructions and perform functions undreamed of before. The production of novel or special-purpose typefaces of limited sales potential was discouraged by prohibitive costs of original matrices for typefounding; in today's photographic era this is no longer so. Most standard typefaces have been adapted to photocomposition, and others have been developed to meet the demands of the new technology. Some of the new ones are self-consciously different in the peculiarities of their construction; in the smaller sizes they are neither legible nor pleasant.

Hand lettering has been almost completely eclipsed by machines which consecutively expose and develop letters from rolls of film containing complete alphabets. Proper letter-spacing is difficult to achieve on such machines, a problem that has been summarily solved by the mindless practice of omitting all spaces between letters. Paste-pot lettering, low cost of film alphabets, and the current demand for novelties account for the appearance of so many weird letter-forms in advertising: revivals from the worst period of nineteenth-century design, Psychedelic and Op Art, hybrids based on computer graphics, and some that cannot be classified or described in a few words. In many of these, legibility has been sacrificed to novelty.

Today, a message, especially in advertising and merchandising, must be instantly noticed, understood or believed, and acted upon. The attention span of the average reader or TV viewer is too short to be carried over into what comes in the next minute. The quick and hard sell is often applied to the merchandising of highly competitive products in supermarkets; the selling appeal of a breakfast cereal or washing powder package outweighs aesthetics. Also, the options of choice between competing products or services are generally so narrow that the success of one over the others depends upon the uniqueness of its presentation—the selling power of the image or the "package."

In advertising, graphic art has been traditionally employed to attract attention—perhaps to please; it must now carry the additional burden of psychological persuasion. The pragmatic approach to advertising and merchandising has greatly increased the importance, but not necessarily the stature, of the art director as a coordinator of graphics. He is expected to employ any device best calculated to carry the message clearly, speedily, and effectively. That this is now done so often by exclusive use of selling copy and photograph appears to be a reflection of advertising's alter-ego, the TV commercial. Many consumer advertisements of today, unlike one of Leyendecker's Arrow Collar ads, are the anonymous productions of a team of specialists: idea man, copy writer, market analyst, art director or layout man, and much more often than not, a photographer.

To one interested in graphic art, this diffusion of effort is depressingly evident in the first half of recent *Annuals* of the Art Directors Club of New York devoted to celebration of TV commercials, copy writers, and consumer campaigns of minimal graphic appeal. The second half, however, is reassuring. In this section the art director or designer proves that when left more to his own devices he can truly function as an orchestrator of graphic images. Editorial, educational, and promotional communication of all sorts exhibit an unprecedented range of versatility in the creative use of photography, illustrative techniques, and typography. The most conspicuous characteristic of contemporary graphic art is the casual or adroit—often witty —way in which totally unrelated styles of art, lettering, and typefaces are mixed together in one design. Contemporary graphic artists draw upon a much more extensive reservoir of fresh ideas and motifs, made readily accessible by the welter of new books on every conceivable aspect of art, design, and the memorabilia of social history. So much graphic art of today looks as though it was fun to do.

During past decades, as the publishing industry expanded, graphic art assumed a more vital role in the merchandising of books. The history of the American book jacket is short and its beginnings obscure, though priority has been claimed for a three-color jacket printed as early as 1845. Use of specially designed jackets gathered momentum after 1914, reaching a peak of graphic excellence around 1950, when the Book Jacket Designers Guild was active and interest in calligraphy as a graphic medium was particularly strong. The purely decorative or interpretive approach to jacket design has now given way to one frankly directed toward advertising the book's usefulness or importance, with large lettering and type predominating.

The fantastic growth of mass paperback publishing is a comparatively recent phenomenon. Millions of people who seldom, if ever, enter a bookstore are offered attractively priced reading matter in supermarkets, drugstores, bus terminals, and other places never before exploited by book publishers. Competition is stiff, display space limited, and slow sellers are quickly replaced by new titles. Attention-grabbing and selling appeal are therefore of prime importance, and paperback cover art has become a lively and fruitful outlet for graphic artists and illustrators. Subliminal color combinations, highly specialized styles of pictorial elements, with eye-catching titles, are carefully coordinated for maximum impact. Record-cover designing, another viable market, was greatly stimulated when hi-fi and huge pop-music sales wakened record companies to the rich potentials of record packaging.

Photography has not only revolutionized typography, printing, and advertising but has profoundly affected other departments of the graphic arts. Magazine covers and posters, long the province of illustrators, have been largely preempted by color photography or by photogenic models, whose every fleeting gesture can be recorded be a hand-held fast camera. Competition with the camera has made the academic style of drawing obsolete, and contemporary illustration has shifted from traditional representation to a more decisive role as a medium for direct communication of ideas, leaning toward pungent social comment in editorial art and closer integration with advertising graphics. The *Annuals* of the Society of Illustrators, published since 1959, clearly show the trend toward the free employment of an infinite variety of techniques and mediums in the modern idiom. In many instances, a drawing can reveal insights and express abstract ideas much more compellingly than can the camera's lens; therein lies the strength and importance of the contemporary illustrator.

New dimensions in education, entertainment, and communication have presented new challenges to the graphic artist. With little time or inclination for verbiage, the majority of people are satisfied with superficialities supplied through pictures and predigested comment. In education, the pictorial or diagrammatic presentation of knowledge makes learning easier and more entertaining. The graphic elucidation of complicated processes and functions in science, biology, and mechanics is a wide field in which expert and artist can work profitably together; also the graphic visualization of abstract data in timetables, charts, and maps. Greatly increased transcontinental travel has made necessary the creation of an entirely new and extensive vocabulary of symbols universally legible on maps, timetables, public buildings, and for directing the flow of traffic and providing vital information for which notices in one or two languages are inadequate.

It is too early to properly assess the influence upon the graphic arts of the "youth culture." We are now reaping the harvest of the baby boom of the post-World War II period. In 1950, there were about 24 million persons between the ages of fourteen and twenty-four in the United States; by 1960 their number had increased to almost 27 million. During the next ten years, 13 million more entered this age bracket, a staggering influx of new minds and energy bent on changing the old order.

With respect to graphic art, new directions first surfaced in the poster art revival of the San Francisco hippie culture and in underground newspapers. The craze for posters and Psychedelic Art spread across the nation; Art Nouveau was rediscovered by youth along with the pleasure of unconventional self expression. Nostalgia was turned into Camp and Pop Art—a new form of Dadaism. And the carnival atmosphere and pageantry of the culture boom has almost obliterated the boundaries between aesthetics and entertainment. Good drawing as a fundamental discipline has been rejected; we now see more illustrations, even in national magazines, that are drawn schematically and with little trace of facility in execution. The pervasiveness of the counterculture is apparent in the calculated atavism adopted by many gifted and successful artists. Much of the newest graphic art is aggressively plebeian, closer to the guts, quite in keeping with our age of sensationalism and mayhem.

307

308

The car card by Paul Rand (306), a miniature poster placed above the heads of seated passengers in subways and buses, must shout its message across busy aisles with maximum visual impact. The Coronet Brandy ads, two of a series that received national acclaim in the middle forties, are based on a common symbol—the brandy snifter—in animated form. The background dot pattern symbolizes effervescence of soda. A combination of ingenious elements contribute to an outstanding success story by Paul Rand. A most effective use of a simple line technique by Ben Shahn (309) distinguishes this CBS advertisement. Morton Goldscholl's wet white hand (310) gives special emphasis to this paint maker's warning sign.

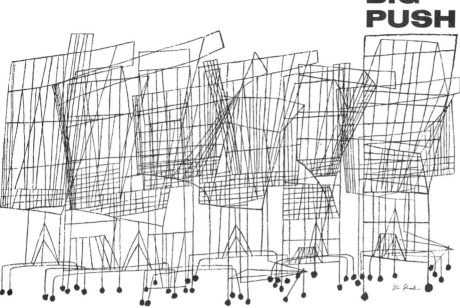

THE BIG PUSH

THIS SUMMER America's consumers will fill their shopping baskets fuller than any summer in their history. And they will fill them with the products they know best — the brands they see on television.

Last summer they spent nearly 10 per cent more than they did the previous winter — 7 per cent more for food; 12 per cent more for household appliances; 15 per cent more in department stores and nearly 8 per cent more on installment purchases.

For the television advertiser, each summer becomes more inviting than the last.

Each summer the average family spends more time watching television.

Each day 8,000 new families join the vast television audience, and by July the number of television homes in the country will total 40,300,000 — nearly 3½ million more than last July.

And each summer CBS Television brings to its advertisers bigger audiences than the summer before and larger than any other network.

CBS Television advertisers are better prepared for the big summer sales push than ever — in fact, this summer 14 per cent more of our winter advertisers will be on the air than a year ago.

These are compelling facts for an advertiser who is debating when or where to launch his new advertising campaign.

Clearly the time to start is now; the place...

CBS TELEVISION

309

WET PAINT MARTIN-SENOUR

Originators of Nu-Hue Colors

310

311

(A ONE ACT PLAY WITH A HAPPY ENDING)

Take it easy, Chief, it isn't three o'clock yet! Those plates are promised at three and *they'll be here at three!* This outfit keeps its promises. Really, it would do your heart good to see their shop. It's the last word in space and equipment. And a bunch of engravers with that good old do or die for Rutgers spirit. Say, with seven swell proof presses they can turn — here comes their boy in the door now. Didn't I tell you, Chief!

Collins, Miller & Hutchings, INC.
Photo-engravers

207 NORTH MICHIGAN AVENUE   CHICAGO

TELEPHONE FRANKLIN 5854

312

HARASSED PRODUCTION MAN. Oh! Oh! The artist who made this is the art director's cousin, and there'll be hell popping if the engraver muffs any of those subtle tones. The printer is the client's brother-in-law, so he will demand super plates and I'll be up creek myself if I don't get quick delivery — the heat is on this job plenty. No chances for me — Operator, get me **FRANKLIN 5854**"

*FRANKLIN 5854 IS THE TELEPHONE NUMBER OF

Collins, Miller & Hutchings, INC., *Photo-engravers*

207 NORTH MICHIGAN AVENUE   CHICAGO

313

Whether your job be a small zinc or a very complex four-color spread, our standard is always the same . . . to make the very finest photoengraving possible.

Collins, Miller & Hutchings, INC.

America's finest photoengraving plant for letterpress and gravure

333 WEST LAKE STREET, CHICAGO

314

mark ye well...

he who neglects his type mark-up will sooner **and** later have to face up to his moment of truth. **Sooner** - for about the time proofs are expected, the typographer might still be setting the job. **Later** - because the bill might have to be high.... And in between are the evil hours of frustration when proofs are wrong and deadlines get nearer and nearer. **So mark ye well** - but don't over-mark. You've selected your typographer because he knows his business." He's part of your team. Show him the effect you want, and he will help you to get it - on time, on the first proof, at the lowest cost. **American Type Founders,** 200 Elmora Avenue, Elizabeth, N. J.   **atf**

Play the exciting new television quiz game that gives the audience at home a chance to win prizes. 11:30 am Monday through Friday live on CBS Television WCBS-TV channel 2

DOTTO

Got plans for a life down on the farm? See what's up for sale by reading the Farm and Acreage ads in The New York Times. Weekdays and Sundays in these Classified Pages.

GIVE YOUR MONEY A LIFT *by starting a Savings Account that earns* **3%** *interest a year at* **THE CHASE MANHATTAN BANK.**
Member Federal Deposit Insurance Corporation

Wit, humor, simplicity of design, and brevity in copy are the bases of many successful advertising messages as shown above: John Averill of Chicago (311–313); William Golden, CBS art director (315); Bill Sokol (316); Howard Wilcox (317). There is obvious symbolism in the simple graphics employed by Saul Bass for the movie ad (318).

319

320

A noted fine artist applies his skilled hand in these specimens with related background motifs. For the cover of *Print* (319), Ben Shahn has combined his crisp, linear drawing in black with the magazine title in red. Using full color, the bold vertical abstract pattern in reds, oranges, and greens is surprinted with the lettered title of the poster in black (320).

Jane Addams

on the basis of civilization

Civilization

is a method

of living,

an attitude

of equal

respect

for all men.

(Speech, Honolulu, 1933)

Container Corporation of America

Artist: George Giusti

For many years the institutional series of advertisements called "Great Ideas of Western Man" has employed the country's most distinguished artists and writers. Seen here is the work of George Giusti (321) and Antonio Frasconi (322).

THERE IS NOTHING MORE FRIGHTFUL THAN IGNORANCE IN ACTION

323

Fine photography comes to the aid of the advertiser in the award-winning wordless message for Kent Cigarettes (323). In the photographic essay (324), visual hyperbole not only stops the eye, but the picture humorously and memorably illustrates the copy which is virtually an irreducible statement in telling and selling.

great sandwiches start and end with
LEVY'S
real Jewish rye

325

326

327

The Daily News employs its photojournalism
expertise in two very convincing advertisements.
The power of graphics (325) needs no extra
wordage—the message is completely in the
picture. Again, the entire story is told in the
copyless poster (326), possibly because it can be
condensed to its primary sales point. The cereal
story could not be better told than with the aid
of three helpful cubs who tell it all (327).

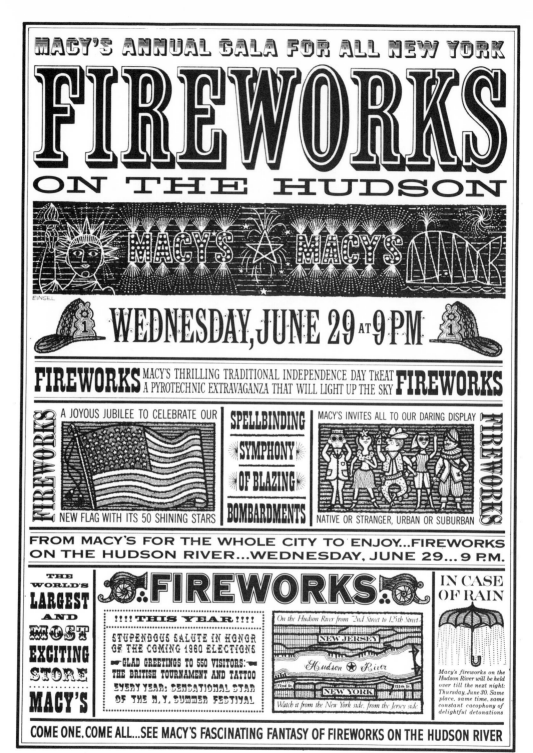

328

329

In the highly competitive field of department store advertising as featured in large newspaper space, the finely rendered line drawings by Walter Einsel combine well with revivalist type and lettering styles to create an intriguing, eye-catching ensemble.

330

331

332

333

ARMISTICE DAY
WINCHESTER CATHEDRAL
THANKSGIVING
LETTERING FIREWORKS
TIJUANA BRASS
CELEBRATION
AMERICA the BEAUTIFUL!
FIREWORKS
BAND · CONCERT · TONIGHT!
MEMORIAL

334

The versatility of film lettering extensively used
in all phases of the graphic arts has been both
a boon to advertisers and a blow to the hand-
letterers, now an almost extinct group.

336

Contemporary graphic designers must be prepared to find expression not only in greatly varied pictorial techniques and typographical arrangements, but in an awareness and response to environmental and sociological concerns. The designer's *oeuvre* can be extremely experimental, often combining drawing, photography, painting, and sculpture to produce startling effects, always within the framework of successful reproduction. Seymour Chwast's work (335–340) runs the gamut of all graphic needs.

196

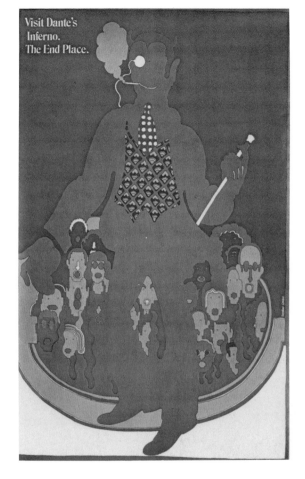

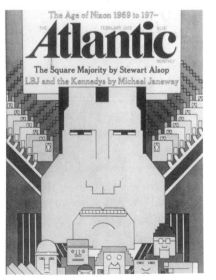

343

Preeminent among the leaders of today's graphic artists, Milton Glaser pursues a wide range of pictorial interests as illustrator, painter, designer, teacher, and co-founder of Push-Pin Studios. The paired posters (341, 342) were planned to make varied display arrangements. An album cover for *Don Giovanni* (343) shows pen-and-ink details; an Art Deco exhibition poster (344); the well-known Dylan poster (345) that has been internationally admired sold over six million copies. Paul Davis, another Push-Pin alumnus (346), works in varied techniques.

Just as the New York School has led the way in abstract-expressionism, so also has an important new direction in poster making been advanced in San Francisco. Deeply influenced by Art Nouveau, the western group distorts composition and lettering in designs now known as Rock Posters. These posters announce rock perform- ances and are also used in dance halls during the performances for atmospheric effects. While all posters have a specific local function they are bought and collected by devotees internationally. Victor Morosco (347) and Wes Wilson (348–351) are the designers.

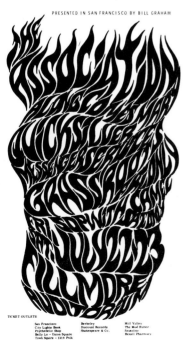

SELECTIVE BIBLIOGRAPHY

General Works and Social History

Adams, James T., Ed., *Album of American History,* New York, 1944.
American Heritage, *American Manners and Morals,* New York, 1969.
Butterfield, Roger, *The American Past,* New York, 1947.
Churchill, Allen, *Remember When: 1900–1942,* New York, 1967.

Book and Magazine Publishing

Brigham, Clarence S., *Journals and Journeymen,* Philadelphia, 1950.
Finley, Ruth E., *Sarah Josepha Hale: The Lady of Godey's,* Philadelphia, 1931.
Kramer, Sidney, *A History of Stone and Kimball,* Chicago, 1940.
Mott, John Luther, *American Journalism, 1690–1950,* New York, 1950.
Mott, John Luther, *A History of American Magazines,* Cambridge, Mass., 1930–1957.
Peterson, Theodore, *Magazines in the Twentieth Century,* Urbana, Ill., 1964.
Tebbel, John, *A History of Book Publishing in the U.S.,* New York, 1972–1974.

Printing History

Bennett, Paul A., *Books and Printing,* New York, 1951.
Cave, Roderick, *The Private Press,* New York, 1971.
Eckman, Dr. James, *The Heritage of the Printer,* Philadelphia, 1965.
Ford, Paul Leicester, *The New England Primer,* New York, 1899.
Grannis, Chandler B., Ed., *Heritage of the Graphic Arts,* New York, 1972.
Kittredge, George Lyman, *The Old Farmer and His Almanac,* Boston, 1904.
Lehmann-Haupt, Hellmut, *The Book in America,* New York, 1939. New Edit., 1952.
Miller, C. William, *Benjamin Franklin's Philadelphia Printing,* Phila., 1974.
Oswald, John Clyde, *Printing in the Americas,* New York, 1937.
Ransom, Will, *Private Presses and Their Books,* New York, 1929.
Shipton, Clifford K., *Isaiah Thomas,* Rochester, New York, 1948.
Silver, Rollo G., *The American Printer, 1787–1825,* Charlottesville, Va., 1967.
Updike: American Printer and His Merrymount Press, New York, 1947.
Wroth, Lawrence C., *The Colonial Printer,* New Edit., Charlottesville, Va., 1964.

Typography and Letter Forms

Ballinger, Raymond A., *Lettering Art in Modern Use,* New York, 1952.
Burns, Aaron, *Typography,* New York, 1961.
Ettenberg, Eugene M., *Type for Books and Printing,* New York, 1947.
Gray, Nicolette, *Nineteenth Century Ornamented Types and Title Pages,* London, 1938.
Hornung, Clarence P., *Lettering From A to Z,* New York, 1946.

Kelly, Rob Roy, *American Wood Type, 1828–1900,* New York, 1969.
Lawson, Alexander, *Printing Types: An Introduction,* Boston, 1971.
Silver, Rollo G., *Typefounding in America, 1787–1825,* Charlottesville, Va., 1965.
Society of Typographic Arts, *The Book of Oz Cooper,* Chicago, 1949.
Tschichold, Jan, *Asymmetric Typography,* London, 1967.

Advertising History

Art Directors Club, The, *Annual of Advertising and Editorial Art,* New York, 1921–.
Clymer, Floyd, *Historical Scrapbook of Early Advertising,* New York, 1955.
Hornung, Clarence P., *Handbook of Early Advertising Art,* 2 vols., New York, 1947.
Presbrey, Frank, *A History of Advertising,* New York, 1929.
Rowsome, Frank, Jr., *They Laughed When I Sat Down,* New York, 1959.
Watkins, Julian Lewis, *The 100 Greatest Advertisements,* New York, 1949.

Design and General Graphics

Allen, Charles Dexter, *American Book Plates,* New York, 1894, Reprint, 1974.
Bauhaus: Weimar, Dessau, Berlin, Chicago, Cambridge, Mass., 1969.
Buday, George, *The History of the Christmas Card,* London, 1954.
Colophon, The, The Annual of Bookmaking, 1927–1937, New York, 1938.
Craig, James, *Production for the Graphic Designer,* New York, 1974.
Glaser, Milton, *Milton Glaser Graphic Design,* New York, 1974.
Graphic Forms: The Arts as Related to the Book, Cambridge, Mass., 1949.
Graphic Designers in the USA, New York, 1971. Vol. 1: *Louis Danziger, Herb Lubalin, Peter Max, Henry Wolf;* Vol. 2: *R. O. Blechman, Chermayeff & Geismar, Paul Davis, Rudolph de Harak;* Vol. 3: *Louis Dorfsman, Milton Glaser, George Tscherny, Tomi Ungerer.*
Hamill, Alfred E., *The Decorative Work of T. M. Cleland,* New York, 1929.
Hechtlinger, Adelaide, *The Great Patent Medicine Era,* New York, 1970.
Hornung, Clarence P., *Old Fashioned Christmas in Illustration and Decoration,* New York, 1970.
Hornung, Clarence P., *Will Bradley: His Graphic Work,* New York, 1974.
Hurlburt, Allan, *Publication Design,* New York, 1971.
Landauer, Bella C., *Early American Trade Cards,* New York, 1927.
Lee, Marshall, Ed., *Books for Our Time,* New York, 1951.
Lee, Ruth Webb, *A History of Valentines,* New York, 1952.
Lewis, John, *Printed Ephemera,* New York, 1962.

Lewis, John, *The Twentieth Century Book,* New York, 1967.
McClinton, Katharine M., *The Chromolithographs of Louis Prang,* New York, 1973.
Munsey, Cecil, *The Illustrated Guide to the Collectibles of Coca Cola,* New York, 1972.
Push Pin Style, The, New York, 1970.
Rand, Paul, *Thoughts on Design,* New York, 1971.
Wilson, Adrian, *The Design of Books,* New York, 1967.

Illustration and Printmaking

Brigham, Clarence S., *Paul Revere's Engravings,* Worcester, Mass., 1954.
Burr, F. M., *Life and Works of Alexander Anderson,* New York, 1893.
Gelman, Barbara, *The Wood Engravings of Winslow Homer,* New York, 1969.
Gelman, Woody, *The Best of Charles Dana Gibson,* New York, 1969.
Goodrich, Lloyd, *The Graphic Art of Winslow Homer,* New York, 1968.
Hamilton, Sinclair, *Early American Book Illustration and Wood Engravers, 1670–1870,* 2 vols., Princeton, N.J., 1968.
Held, John, Jr., The Most of, Brattleboro, Vt., 1972.
Illustrators, The Society of, *The Illustrators Annual,* New York, 1959–.
Jussim, Estelle, *Visual Communication and the Graphic Arts,* New York, 1974.
Ludwig, Coy, *Maxfield Parrish,* New York, 1973.
Mayor, A. Hyatt, *Popular Prints of the Americas,* New York, 1973.
Meyer, Susan, *James Montgomery Flagg,* New York, 1974.
Peters, Harry T., *America on Stone,* New York, 1931.
Pitz, Henry C., *The Gibson Girl and Her America,* New York, 1969.
Pitz, Henry C., *Howard Pyle,* New York, 1975.
Pratt, John Lowell, *Currier & Ives: Chronicles of America,* Maplewood, N.J., 1968.
Schau, Michael, *J. C. Leyendecker,* New York, 1974.
Weitenkampf, Frank, *American Graphic Art,* New York, 1924.

Posters

Breitenbach, Edgar, *The Poster Craze,* New York, 1962.
Cirker, Hayward and Blanche, *The Golden Age of the Poster,* New York, 1971.
Darracott, Joseph, *The First World War in Posters,* New York, 1974.
Hutchinson, Harold F., *The Poster: An Illustrated History From 1860,* New York, 1968.
Metzl, Ervine, *The Poster, Its History and Its Art,* New York, 1963.
Price, C. Matlack, *Poster Design,* New York, 1913.
Walker, Cummings G., *The Great Poster Trip: Eureka,* Palo Alto, Calif., 1968.

INDEX